FOR TEENS & YOUNG ADULTS: SETTING AND ACHIEVING GOALS THAT MATTER TO ME

Jennifer Leigh Youngs, A.A. · Bettie Burres Youngs, Ph.D., Ed.D.

from the SMART TEENS-SMART CHOICES series

Teen Town Press
www.TeenTownPress.com

an imprint of Bettie Youngs Book Publishers, Inc.

BETTIE YOUNGS BOOKS

Cover Graphic Design: Adrian Pitariu and Beau Kimbrel
Text Design: Beau Kimbrel
Editorial Consultant: Gerald L. Kuiper
Text Consultant: Jennifer Leigh Youngs
Teen Consultant: Kendahl Brooke Youngs

TEEN TOWN PRESS / www.TeenTownPress.com
Teen Town Press is an Imprint of **Bettie Youngs Book Publishing Co., Inc.:**
www.BettieYoungsBooks.com.

If you are unable to order this book from your local bookseller or online, you may order directly from the publisher: info@BettieYoungsBooks.com.

Print ISBN: 978-1-940784-97-7
Digital ISBN: 978-1-940784-96-0

10 9 8 7 6 5

Library of Congress Cataloging-in-Publication Data Available upon Request.

Youngs, Bettie, Youngs, Jennifer.
FOR TEENS & YOUNG ADULTS: Setting and Achieving Goals that Matter TO ME
Summary: Stories, commentary, skills and advice for young adults for setting and achieving goals. 1. Achievement and motivation in adolescence.—YA literature. 2. Setting and Achieving Goals— [1. Self-Help for daily life. 2. Daily Living. 3. Success. 4. Psychology. 5. Bettie Youngs, Ph.D., Ed.D. 6. Jennifer L. Youngs, A.A.]

Also by the Authors for Teens and Young Adults

TEENS & YOUNG ADULTS: How Your Brain Decides If You Will Become Addicted—Or Not

TEENS & YOUNG ADULTS: Setting and Achieving Goals that Matter TO ME

TEENS & YOUNG ADULTS: Managing the Stress, Pressure and the Ups and Downs of Life

TEENS & YOUNG ADULTS: The 10 Commandments and the Secret Each One Guards—FOR YOU

TEENS & YOUNG ADULTS: The Power of Being Kind, Courteous and Thoughtful

TEENS & YOUNG ADULTS: How to Be Courageous

TEENS & YOUNG ADULTS: How to Have a Great Attitude

TEENS & YOUNG ADULTS: Understanding the Christian Faith

TEENS & YOUNG ADULTS: Growing Your Confidence and Self-Esteem

TEENS & YOUNG ADULTS: Caring for Your Body's Health and Wellness

TEENS & YOUNG ADULTS: What I Learned About Love (So Far)

TEENS & YOUNG ADULTS: Friends

TEENS & YOUNG ADULTS: Having Healthy and Beautiful Hair, Skin and Nails

TEENS & YOUNG ADULTS: Daily Inspiration

TEENS & YOUNG ADULTS: Faith at Work in Your Life

TEENS & YOUNG ADULTS: Inspirational Stories and Encouragement on Friends and the Face in the Mirror

CONTENTS

OTHER BOOKS BY TEEN TOWN PRESS

CHAPTER 1
Setting and Achieving Goals That Matter TO YOU

This book is for teens and young adults and is filled with advice on how to set and achieve goals. There are stories and commentary by young people, ages twelve to twenty, who share their ideas and tell of their experiences about the importance of setting and achieving goals.

As most teens know, goals spell the difference between wishful thinking and making things happen. As 16-year-old Breanna Hillard explained: *"Of all my friends, the most 'exciting' are the ones who make things happen—and to do that, you've got to set goals. An example that comes to mind is when, just recently, a band I love was coming to town. Everyone at school was like, 'Oh, it's going to be the best concert; we've just got to get tickets!' The tickets were very expensive, and the word got around that the concert would be sold out within hours of tickets going on sale.*

I knew straight away that those who made being at the concert their goal lost no time in getting permission from their parents, and earning the money they needed, buying the tickets and organizing a ride to and from the concert. I've learned that people who decide on something and then set a goal to bring it about are the ones who achieve what they want. To me, those who set and achieve goals are the most fun to be around. They're very exciting, and very cool."

As Breanna makes clear, setting goals and reaching them means you're likely to be among those who get to enjoy the rewards.

When was the last time you and your friends talked about the most important goals each of you have? Maybe you answered that question something like this: "Just last week my friends and I talked about our plans to ace the semester finals," or "With the prom coming up, we talked about how we could organize enough of our friends to chip in and pay for a limo." Or, maybe upon reading the question you chuckled and said, "Talking about goals is a geeky thing to do, and none of my friends do it!"

Think about it. You and your friends may not sit down to the lunch table and say, "Okay, let's all talk about our goals," but that doesn't mean you don't discuss the things that you'd like or plan to do, whether for the immediate future, like this weekend, or in the distant future, like two years from now. Even a (daily, weekly or monthly) "to-do" list is an indication you have goals. Do you and your friends talk about your goals?

What Young People Say Are Reasons They Talk About Their Goals

Teens who do discuss their goals with each other say they do so because of one or more of the following reasons:

- All my friends talk about what's important to them.
- The more I talk about what I'd like to do, the more I find out, for sure, what is important to me, as well as what is not. This clarity helps me make decisions.
- Talking about the things I want to do helps me commit to achieving them.
- I When I talk about my plans with my friends (and parents and teachers, too), I get a lot of information on how to make my dreams even better or bigger. And I often learn how to do things in a better or more efficient way than when I'm left to my own thinking.
- Talking about my goals makes me feel important and like a "somebody" with my friends and family.
- Talking about my goals makes me feel like my life is going well, like I'm not wasting my time. And I like how I feel about myself when I'm achieving things that are important to me.

What Young People Say Are Reasons They Do NOT Discuss Their Goals

As you can see, it's good to talk about your goals. Talking about what's important to you is a first step in discovering and clarifying who you are and what you want out of day-to-day life and for the "future" as well. Setting goals that are important to you, and formulating a plan of action to achieve your goals, will help you commit to action to achieve them. More on this later, but here are primary reasons young people say they do not discuss their goals with others, with commentary.

- I'm not sure what I want to do and don't want to be lacking ambition.

    Commentary: Probably that's a good reason to set goals—at least those that help you explore your interests, hobbies and aptitudes. In this book, you'll get a chance to explore who you are and what you want. You'll learn how to devise a plan to uncover, little by little, those things that make you excited about taking more and more control of your life, as well as plan to have a bigger say in shaping the direction of life—both for the days and years ahead. You'll also get a chance to set goals in nine specific areas, a feat that is sure to leave you feeling that you are not without ambition.

- With my friends, it's just not cool to talk about goals

  Commentary: Some teens may believe it's not "cool" to talk about their goals, but nothing could be further from the truth. It's very cool to be involved in your life and take an active role in shaping the way your days, weeks, months and years unfold. Look around you; you'll find that many teens are actively pursuing their dreams and ambitions—and whether they speak out loud or let their achievements do the talking, teens with goals are not wallflowers!

- I don't want to risk that others might belittle, ridicule or discourage me in meeting my goals.

  Commentary: It's true that someone may—even with good intentions—discourage you from attempting your goals. Maybe this person believes you've set your expectations too high, believing that the goals you want to achieve are too difficult for you, and that you'll fail to meet your goal as a result. And, of course, someone could tell you (perhaps out of jealousy) that your chances of meeting your goals are "ridiculous" or "preposterous"! Share your goals anyway. It won't be long before you silence the doubts of "naysayers"— as well as develop the confidence in yourself to not get sidetracked by comments that belittle, ridicule and discourage you from tackling your goals.

- I don't want to set myself up for failure: If I said I wanted to accomplish something, and then didn't, I'd look, and feel, bad.

  Commentary: What if you tell everyone your goal is to get on the pep squad, and you try out but don't make the team? Of course, in the hours and days that follow, your having not made the team will be a disappointment to you. That's only natural. And there will be those who feel, as you do, disappointed. And some will feel sad for you, and there just may be a person or two who is pleased that you didn't make the team. But you did something—you "went for it"! Seldom does anyone meet 100 percent of his or her goals in life. But as an old saying goes, "**You always miss 100 percent of the shots** you don't take!" Go for it! Know that you'll survive and can even thrive during those times you don't succeed. And there is something else you should consider: Most people will not fault you for trying to succeed at your goals, even if you don't hit your mark in the end.

•   I'm not all that clear on how to go about setting goals.

    <u>Commentary:</u> Probably this isn't true. If, for example, you say, "I'm going to get all of my homework done this week!," that's a goal! You don't have to save the rain forest in order to qualify as having a goal. A decision and plan to pass this week's test, or to stop biting your nails, or to develop a better relationship with a family member, all qualify as goals. And here's some more good news: This book will help you learn a great deal about setting and achieving goals!

"You always miss 100 percent of the shots you don't take!"

Talking about your goals is a good thing! Clarifying what you'd like to "do, have, be and achieve" is one of the best ways to have a fun, interesting and rewarding life. Everyone needs to look forward to doing purposeful things. If you have no goals whatsoever, you might feel that life is boring, even depressing. Having goals means you are actively participate in creating the life you want. The first step is knowing yourself, and then actively setting goals to have the life you want.

In this book you'll meet young people who readily discuss their goals, from small ones to grand ones, from seemingly lighthearted ones to serious ones, from lifelong dreams to recent ones. You'll find stories from those whose goals focus on immediate problems—such as the teen who had the misfortune of losing his pet snake, to teens who have been working toward a goal for a long time. Whether centered on relationships, school, hobbies or sports, setting goals makes it more likely you'll achieve those things that are important to you.

As you read each story, you'll discover that whether teens call their goals "baby steps" or "Eiffel Tower plans," they see them as building blocks for having a fun life that is interesting and fulfilling. As you read about their ambitions, be thinking about the goals that are most important to you both now and in the future. Then, throughout the remainder of this book, we'll show you how to map out a plan and set a steady course for achieving your own goals that are important to you—and worthy of you!

CHAPTER 2

TEEN TALK: How I Learned What Was Important to Me

Here are some stories by young people who tell how they began to see their interests emerging. As you read each one, think about if you were asked to do the same, what you would write.

Is That Eddie Murphy Under All That Makeup?

My eyes were glued to the screen—she looked like she was nearly a hundred years old—but she was only in her twenties! Maybe you remember seeing this sort of incredible transformation of a screen character. Take Eddie Murphy, for example. He can play his handsome self in one scene, and in the very next, a very old Caucasian lady! Sitting there in the theater and seeing this remarkable change—and knowing it's Eddie Murphy—you still find yourself asking, "Is that really Eddie Murphy?" And it's all done at the hands of a very skilled makeup artist.

I find the art—and magic—of makeup amazing. I'm so intrigued by how someone who is old is suddenly transformed into someone young, and how someone very young can look old (and all the ages in between). It's just amazing to me that someone attractive can play an ugly monster; a young man can appear to be an old woman; a woman can appear to be a man; and a man can look like the most feminine woman. What incredible illusions—and all due, largely, to makeup artistry. Seeing it all leaves me with this "I have to do that" feeling. And so, it's become a goal: I'd like to be a makeup artist.

I don't have it all worked out as to how I'm going to reach my goal, but I'm working on it. I can only tell you that excitement fills me even when I walk near a makeup counter in a department store, most especially if there's a makeup artist showing someone how to artfully apply makeup.

I guess you could say I've been interested in makeup for a long time. My mother tells me that as a child, I was always into her cosmetics and wanting to put on lipstick, eyeliner, perfume—and everything else! All my friends are always asking me to do their makeup for them when they have a special date, are going to the prom or want to look "very cool." They tell me that I do it so well and always say things like, "Wow—it's beautiful!" or, "It looks so professionally done."

5

But like I said, I'm just getting things figured out on how to reach my bigger goal. I know that I'm going to start out by going to beauty school and get a cosmetology license. Then I'd like to get some experience working in a great department store with a classy makeup department. After that, I think I'd like to contact some local television stations and see if I can become the makeup artist for the on-air TV personalities. (I think it would be so cool to get a job as the makeup artist with a big television star, like be Oprah's makeup person!) After that, I'll see if I can work in local theater. I plan to do all this so that I can have some good experience "under my belt," then I plan to move on to—well, who knows, maybe I'll be a "special-effects makeup artist" on a movie set. It would be so totally cool to work on a movie in the caliber of Lord of the Rings! And I just may—hey, you never know!

So those are my plans to date. I know that working in the motion-picture industry is going to mean I'll need good experience as well as some good contacts in order to get "my foot in the door." So far, I don't have any, but I must start somewhere, and I plan to. A few years from now, when you're watching the latest and greatest special-effects movie, try to remember not to leave the theater before the final credits roll, because that's where you'll see my name! —Colette Feener, 16

Call Me "Dr. Santos"

When I was seven years old, I was hospitalized for spinal meningitis. While I was there, the head doctor on my treatment team, Dr. Hazelton, not only saved my life, but also was really kind to me. Every day, he took the time to make me smile and was always exceptionally friendly. He never treated me like I was too young to understand what it meant to have spinal meningitis and what he planned to do to treat it. He also didn't think I was too young to have an opinion about my treatment. That made me feel very special and as the doctor liked to say, "an important part of the treatment team." I really believe all of this was important to my getting well.

It certainly was a big factor in my goal to become a doctor when I got better and finished school. I knew I wanted to be the same sort of doctor—knowledgeable, friendly and respectful of his patients. Then for a long time, I forgot all about it, until I was in high school and it was time to decide what classes I needed to take in order to get into a college program. This forced me to think about what I was going to do with my life. I knew I wanted to help people. And in remembering the doctor who healed me, I decided practicing medicine would be a wonderful way to use my life. I renewed my desire to be a doctor.

I believe it's good to visualize myself doing what I hope for most in life, so now I picture myself in a white coat with a stethoscope hanging around my neck, my diploma on the wall, and being able to help and heal others. Remembering my doctor and his kindness, as well as how he healed me by being a great physician, gives me a perfect role model for moving toward my goal. My excitement for being a doctor is at an all-time high.

Being a doctor and healing others are what I hope for most in life. It's what sets the mark I aim for in my grades, and what guides me in the classes I choose. When I go out for sports, I ask myself if I can do that without it getting in the way of my studies—which will take me to my goal to be a doctor. I even turned down a job at the video store because I'd have to commit to too many hours. Instead, I took a job with fewer hours in the hospital cafeteria. Besides, being in that setting keeps me focused on becoming a doctor, which is the goal that I'm striving for most. —Craig Santos, 18

"Stop Gnawing on Those Fingernails!"

I have been biting my nails for as long as I can remember. Until two years ago, it didn't really bother me, although it made my mother furious. She's been trying to get me to stop since I've been a little kid. Nothing she tried worked, and believe me, she tried a lot of things, from wiping my fingers with rubbing alcohol (which has a nasty taste!) to gloves taped to my wrists (which are very difficult to chew off or pull off, given that your hands are out of commission). Like I said, none of her tactics were successful in getting me to stop gnawing on my nails.

Then, when I entered ninth grade, I noticed that many of the girls had pretty nails, and I decided it was time to have nice-looking nails, too. I decided I'd stop biting my nails. Well, breaking the habit of biting your nails is not an easy one—as anyone who bites his or her nails will tell you. That year, I tried a million things to stop. I dipped my fingers in all sorts of bitter concoctions, from hot sauces to offensive gels manufactured for this very purpose. I've bandaged my fingertips, and I've even glued on false nails, hoping that chewing on hard plastic would be a turn-off. No luck! Like my mother's attempts to get me to stop biting my nails, my methods met with very little success as well.

Until a month ago. Under the most embarrassing of situations, I found the motivation to stop biting my nails.

If your school is anything like mine, there are about four "levels" of popular kids. There are the brainy types—always respected at our school, but the thing is, you have to practically be a genius to be "one of the crowd" so it's easier just to admire this group and think they're cool. The second group is the athletes, which, let's face it, is yet another type of genius—body agility. I'm all feet and couldn't and wouldn't trek around the track thirty laps, or be seen running through town, for anything.

So, like the brainy types, those of us who are not gifted with muscles who insist on going for a jog around the world every day, well, we just admire and think this group is cool, too. Then, there are the nerds—and who wants to be a nerd? The fourth group is the social elite, those who have a way to make the rest of us just feel, well, socially inept, but wishing we weren't. I long to be in this group—specifically, I've wanted to be noticed (and invited to hang out) by Janelle Rosen, considered the "most cool" girl in the class, and Rochelle Watson, considered the most popular girl in the school. Janelle and Rochelle were always nice enough, but never really "noticed" me, if you know what I mean. Then, a few weeks ago at an all-school talent show, I ended up sitting right beside them, and all that changed! Can you believe the luck?

Our school's talent show is a cool event, and like everyone else, I was looking forward to it. So that I'd look cool that day, I'd borrowed my sister's red sweater, since "color charts" indicate I'm a "winter" and red is supposed to be a really good color for me (which I think must be true because every time I wear red, I get nice compliments). I even had my sister help with my hair. She's eighteen and has learned a lot about how to blow- dry hair so it looks awesome. I looked great, if I do say so myself—well, all except for my nails. As usual, I'd bitten them as far down as you can imagine, so I hadn't even bothered putting polish on them—I mean, it's practically a waste of time, and sometimes when I do polish them, it seems to me that it only makes the fact that they are barely there even more obvious. Oh, well, I'd just keep them in my pockets.

Here I was at the talent show, sitting right beside Miss Cool and Miss Popular, thinking things couldn't get any better. I mean, everyone always noticed Janelle and Rochelle; even being seen with them elevated your "must be cool, too" status.

At our school's talent show, the drama teacher, who is always "host," chooses two judges from the faculty, two from student council and two students in the audience. "Who wants to judge?" Mr. Fitzhugh shouted as the student filming the talent show scanned the room and then zoomed in on a face every few seconds and projected the person on the big screen on the stage of the auditorium. Well, there were about a billion kids with their hands in the air cheering and begging to be chosen as the judge. The whole auditorium was filled with this air of excitement and you could only imagine mine, sitting here in the row with Miss Cool and Miss Popular. I watched every move Janelle and Rochelle made, hoping to catch their eyes and flash them a friendly smile. Then suddenly, all got quiet for like an instant, and then everyone started laughing, hooting and howling. I looked around and everyone's eyes were glued to the screen in the front of the room. I stopped looking at the crowd and turned to look at the screen up front. There, larger than life on the huge monitor at the top of the stage, was my image, gnawing on my nails like a deranged and starving rodent who had finally run across a morsel of food. This, in front of the entire school! Worse, I was practically sitting in the laps of Janelle and Rochelle. I was mortified! Even more so when the drama teacher said, "Well then, stop gnawing on those nails, Ms. Kelly, and come on up here." I got out of my seat and made my way to the front of the auditorium, my face as red as my sweater.

I am determined to work on my goal: I am absolutely, positively going to stop biting my nails—starting this very moment! —**Kelly Harris, 15**

My Wild, Wild Imagination

As a kid, I had a really, wild imagination. My mind created one fascinating world after another, and each time, expanded on a previous adventure, the plot thickening. The world of the calculating Professor Canard and his debonair archnemesis—The Martini Penguin—was my most favorite "mental playground." With the help of Professor Canard, I traveled throughout the world, foiling the latest diabolical plot of The Martini Penguin. The adventures of Professor Canard ranged from the "Maltese Penguin" to "The Susceptibles" (take-offs on the movies Maltese Falcon and The Untouchables).

By the time I got to be a teen, the world of Professor Canard was replaced by flashy video games and electronic wonders. Though they dazzled my senses, they never compared to the rich imaginary world I'd created as a kid. Being a mere shadow of the indomitable, imaginative giant of my youth, they couldn't replace my world with its former glory. Luckily, things are changing. Two years ago, I took an extension college course in computer animation. The course taught how to three-dimensionally animate anything. Using the tools learned in the class, I began to experiment with creating different worlds. But then I remembered my childhood creation of Professor Canard. I began to model basic shapes and slowly transform them into the characters I imagined. The joy of seeing dreams made reality is incredible!

When I was a child, my vivid imagination provided all the "invisible visibles," but now, I want to see my world in real time, played out exactly how I imagine it. To do this I have to find innovative and exciting tools to assist my mind in reinstating Professor Canard, which is just one of my many goals. I've tried working with clay as my tool toward this goal, but it just wasn't right for me. When working with clay, it's quite unnerving to watch your creation collapse into a pile of mush. Another frustrating quandary with clay is the kiln. Finally, you have shaped a beautiful clay pot that has your heart and soul in it, but a tiny air bubble within the clay causes your creation to literally explode within the fiery inferno of the kiln. In 3-D animation, this can never happen. Physics are turned off when working with "digital clay," and there is no risk of explosion. I believe the appeal of computer animation comes from the ability to work, uninhibited by physics, in a world of your own design.

What began as my wild imagination has turned into my greatest ambition, and that is to be able to turn this hobby into a career of work in 3-D animation. It's something that attracts and holds me like nothing else. Using my imagination to bring a world with self-contained characters and life into being is positively thrilling. So, by combining two things I enjoy most—computers and art—I'm going to create a career in animation for myself. Little did I know that what I used to amuse me and escape the monotony of general boredom as a kid, would become the "brainchild" behind my goals today, goals that are no longer beyond my wildest imagination! —Thomas Hatfield, 16

"Royce's Little Sister"? Oh, Please!

I am in ninth grade, and my brother Royce is a senior. He's cool and has a lot of friends. All the teachers like him. None of this interfered with my life until this school year. Now that I'm attending school on the same campus as he does, I seem to have lost my identity. When I was in junior high, everything was fine: I felt like a real person, an individual with a personality of my own. But now, suddenly, I seem to be reduced to being seen only as a "sister"—"Royce's sister." It's a real drag. The other day I raised my hand in class with an answer to a question, and after answering it correctly, the teacher remarked, "Oh, you're as smart as your brother!" In PE class I was told, "Athleticism must run in your family." Plus, Royce is a regular comedian, always witty and sees the humor in any situation. So, everyone keeps expecting me to be funny, too—which I'm not. But who knows, I might be funny if I weren't under such pressure to be. But it was no laughing matter in the cafeteria when I ran into Mike Larson, a guy I have a huge crush on. Naturally when I saw him, I smiled, and he smiled back at me. Then the friend with him teased him, saying, "Oh, got a thing for Royce's little sister, huh?" I cringed, knowing that being someone's "little sister" is the kiss of death as far as romance goes.

Royce this and Royce that! It's been more than a couple of months now, and it's gone on long enough! His going to this school and being so well-known affects every area of my life. So, my goal this year is to be a personality in my own right, to be Marissa Farintini and not "Royce's sister." My plan is to look different and act different. For starters, I'm going to put a fuchsia rinse in my hair. It's a very cool look, and the opposite of Royce's "preppy" looks. Hopefully, even though it may sound like a baby step, this will help set me apart and stamp me with a personality of my own. Because quite frankly, I just do not want to be identified as "Royce's little sister" anymore. Having my own identity is a goal I intend to achieve—and the sooner, the better! —**Marissa Farintini, 14**

Shutting Out Jackson-Brown

When I was twelve, my parents got me a puppy, a Pom-Poo (part Pomeranian and part poodle). I named him Jackson-Brown because my last name is Brown, and my dad loves the music of Jackson Brown, so I've listened to his music at home all my life. While I liked the music, I loved my puppy Jackson-Brown.

And it was easy to tell that he loved me. He slept in my room at the end of my bed. Jackson-Brown would moan softly when I left for school in the morning or for a soccer game on the weekend, and he'd be right there by the door to greet me when I got home. It was so sweet! He'd be so happy to see me that he'd turn around and around, sometimes getting himself so excited that he would pee on himself (and on the floor)! That part wasn't so sweet, since I had to clean up after him. But I loved him anyway. He was great—just a little dog that wanted to be with me in everything I did. I'm sure he thought of us as a twosome. He liked my parents all right, but he loved me.

Last year I started making more friends, and they would come over to my house after school. I'm sure Jackson-Brown decided that if these were friends of mine, they'd be friends of his, too. When my friends came over, Jackson-Brown would run in, thrilled that "he and I" had company and jump all over everything. Sometimes my friends and I would have clothes laid out on the bed (or homework) and he'd be dancing all over them. And if we had any food, of course, he'd want to eat it. I always had to chase him out and shut the door to my room so he wouldn't interrupt us. I'm sure he felt abandoned, and he'd give me a pathetic "sad eyes" look. I'm sure that he thought it would work; it often did. But sometimes, I just wanted to be alone with my friends, especially if a "new" friend came over and I wanted to get to know her—and have her think I was cool. I mean, not everyone likes other people's pets. And, of course, with Jackson-Brown, he thought he was the attraction! No self-esteem problems there!

One night I had four girls come to my house for an overnight stay. We were playing music and baking pizzas in the kitchen. You can only imagine how happy and excited Jackson-Brown was with all this commotion. In fact, he was irritating me, and I just wasn't in the mood to deal with him. I opened the door and commanded him to go outside. He looked at me with those sad eyes, as though apologizing. With his head lowered to the floor, as if saying, "I'm sorry and sad," he sulked out the door. Then I shut Jackson-Brown outside of the house so he wouldn't get in our way.

Though he had never left our front yard before, Jackson- Brown decided to leave the yard this night. About an hour after my forcing him out of the house, I began to feel kind of guilty and went to let him back in, but he wasn't there on the porch like I expected him to be—nor was he anywhere in the yard. "Jackson!" I called, and then whistled for him, but he didn't come running. I called and called for him, and still he didn't come. Starting to panic, I got my parents and friends to help me, and we set out with flashlights, all of us calling his name and looking for him, but he was nowhere to be found. Finally, my dad called off the search and said, "It's time for you girls to go to bed. We'll try again in the morning." My mom said, "Maybe he'll come home by himself before then."

I was so worried, I could hardly sleep that night; all I could think about was my dog and how much he loved to jump up on my bed to be with me, especially if he could sense that I was feeling stressed out over something, like an argument with a friend. He always knew how to read me. If I was mumbling over a having to take a big test, he'd jump around all happy, begging me to take him for a walk. He was just so sensitive—what a great dog. And the thing with my friends, well, he just wanted to be part of the fun. I just wished I'd had more patience with the poor little thing.

I don't know when I finally fell asleep that night, but I'm sure it was almost dawn. Still groggy, I woke up to the sound of scratching at the back door. Suddenly, I realized what I was hearing, and my eyes popped open and I jumped from the bed. I ran to the back door and opened it, but it was just my imagination. There was no Jackson-Brown pouncing and wiggling and wagging his tail, happy to see me.

We still haven't found Jackson-Brown, and it's been two days now. I put up signs, but no one has called. I'm working on a flyer with his picture on it, and I plan to have them ready tomorrow. Finding him is my number-one goal. I've gone door-to-door throughout the neighborhood. I went to the pound yesterday and plan to go again tomorrow. I've called the Humane Society and on the way to school check to make sure the signs are still up. I'm placing an ad in the "Lost and Found" section of the newspaper tomorrow. I'm a girl with a lot of goals, but right now none seem as important as finding my dog. — Jensen Brown, 13

> ### Goals spell the difference between wishful thinking, and making things happen.

What's Important to You?

Are you beginning to see yourself as having interests come into focus? Just as you read about other young people who told us of a time when this was happening for them, write about a time when you learned what was important to you.

_____

_____

_____

_____

_____

_____

_____

_____

_____

_____

_____

What are Your Most Important Goals Right Now? List five goals that are important to you right now:

1. _____

_____

2. _____

_____

3. _____

_____

4. _____

_____

5. _____

_____

CHAPTER 3

Who Are You?: Setting Goals That Are "Totally You"

When you read the goals and aspirations of young people in the previous stories, were you surprised to learn that goals could apply to so many areas of life and in so many ways? Whether the goal is to change the world or to deepen your own understanding of yourself, whether to discover or uncover your interests, talents and hobbies or to make the honor roll, looking and planning ahead—hoping, wishing, wanting, dreaming—are all phases of setting goals for creating the life you wish to have.

There is a difference, of course, between "wishing, wanting and hoping" and "making your dreams come true." Setting goals is the key. There are so many activities (and distractions) that take up your time. Having goals is the biggest difference between those who accomplish a great deal (or who are on their way to doing so) and those who profess to want to achieve certain things but never seem to make them happen.

Achievers focus their time, task by task by task, to accomplish their mission.

Setting and Achieving Goals Is an Important Formula for Success

Goals point you in the direction of where you should focus your time and energy. By channeling your efforts in a specific direction and on specific tasks or activities, you are more likely to achieve those things you want to accomplish. Heading in the direction you wish to go increases your chances of getting there. Best of all, feeling that you're making strides toward accomplishing those things you'd like to "do, have and be" is a good feeling—and an empowering one.

Having a happy and satisfying life both now and in the future is largely about doing those things that are interesting and important to you. But first you must have some idea of what is interesting and important to you—your needs, values and aspirations. We can be unique in what we want, as you no doubt gathered in the earlier stories by young people. While one teen may wish to become president of his or her class, another may wish to be the person behind the scenes helping that person get elected president. While one person may choose to focus his or her life solely on raising a family, another may wish to focus time and energy on the care and nurturing of animals.

While one person may retreat to the desert to conserve and preserve the natural resources of our environment, another may choose self-expression via the arts or by developing his or her athletic prowess.

YOUR PERSONALITY, APTITUDES AND HOBBIES SAY A GREAT DEAL ABOUT "WHO YOU ARE"

Your personality, aptitudes and hobbies tell a lot about who you are. What does yours reveal about you? How can you make the most of them? Let's examine these areas more closely.

<u>Your Personality</u>: Some say that our personality is an innate (inborn) part of who we are. As such, our personality isn't something that changes a great deal. For example, if you are a gregarious person, you're outgoing and not shy. Probably you like to be with people and therefore prefer doing activities where others are involved, as opposed to doing tasks all by yourself. "Who you are" information is incredibly important in helping you make decisions about what sort of life and lifestyle you'd like. It is also an important consideration in choosing what career might be right for you, even what "regimen" of activities you're more likely to stay with in meeting your goals to be healthy and stay fit.

Who you are is revealed in the clothes you wear, in those hobbies and activities in which time seems to pass quickly, and in the types of friends with whom you most enjoy spending your time. All this is useful information that you can use to set goals to get your life, lifestyle, leisure, work and personal needs met.

Let's say you're wondering how you can incorporate your personality in choosing a career most feasible for you. If you don't like to be outdoors, it is unlikely you will want to apply to be a firefighter or a conservationist. If you love being outdoors, and if you love nature and working with animals, then you may want to consider work that allows you to do that, and to pass up a job that demands that you be in an office all day, working with facts and figures on the computer. If, on the other hand, you really like working with people, especially helping people work through problems, then you may not want to consider being a veterinarian, unless of course, you work primarily in the front office, talking and interacting with the pet owners.

Take a moment now to describe your personality.
I would describe my personality like this:_____

_____

_____

_____

Your Aptitudes: Our strengths, the areas in which we learn most easily, are different for each of us. Perhaps you've always had a talent for writing great letters and stories, and it comes easy to find the right words for any report. On the other hand, your best friend must really work at any written assignment, yet she never forgets anything that is laid out as a picture in front of her, like a map. This is because we each have different aptitudes.

Coming up, you will learn about nine types of intelligence. Rarely, if ever, does anyone have a "high" aptitude in more than two or three of these nine areas. The goal is to find which two or three come naturally, and therefore easily, for you. In the pages ahead you'll get a chance to discover which are your best aptitudes, and learn how to set goals that allow you to lead from your strengths.

Your Hobbies: Because your hobbies display your talents and natural skills and interests, they're also a great source of information about "who you are." And, because our hobbies allow us to uncover our talents and interests, they bring about joy and satisfaction within us. This information can be useful beyond our own inner contentment. While you may think of your hobbies as "just for fun," they can point you in the direction of an exciting job or career goals, and help you set goals to develop friendships with others who share your passions! In the chapters ahead, you'll get a chance to explore your innate interests and set goals that allow further exploration.

Right now, my primary hobby is:_____

_____

_____

_____

The things that interest me the most, right now, include:_____

_____

_____

_____

   Pretty exciting stuff! Understanding your personality and knowing more about your aptitudes and interests, will help you think through who you are and how you can incorporate your set goals for achieving them.

   So, who are you? Have you thought about what you want out of life? Do you have a plan for getting it? This book will help you get more clarity on those answers, which is a terrific step in setting those goals that will help you feel fulfilled, achieved, and good about yourself.

CHAPTER 4

Setting Goals That Are in Sync with Your PERSONALITY

Robin Williams: "A Pain in the Butt"

In his acceptance speech for winning an Academy Award for his performance in a motion picture, Oscar-winner Robin Williams thanked several people, including some high school teachers. "Some of my teachers thought I was 'a pain in the butt,'" he laughed, referring to himself as a jokester, a funny bone who could always see the humor in things as a teenager. Then, clutching his Oscar and growing serious, one of America's most beloved comics remarked, "but one special teacher said to me, 'I hope you'll channel that talent. You'd make a good public speaker!'"

Most people have heard of the late actor and comedian Robin Williams, a man who has certainly succeeded at tailoring his career to fit his personality. Consider the importance and joy of letting your personality shine in all that you do. Of course, you'll need to have a good sense of who you are. Robin Williams had a good sense of himself. We'll bet that if he had ever been asked to identify some of his personality traits, probably he listed things like: "I love to be with people; I love to be funny; I love to be outrageous; I love to make people laugh; I love to study people, to see what makes them tick. Stuff like that." No doubt Robin knew all the things that made him Robin Williams.

How fortunate that Robin's teacher encouraged him to recognize his personality traits and to consider them strengths and coached him to do something with them. It was to be the start of something very special. As his Academy Award confirms, the "pain in the butt" found a way to fashion his personality into a very brilliant success!

"Who" Are You?

How about you? What is your personality, and what does it say about you? Here's a chance to take a closer look!

UNDERSTANDING YOUR PERSONALITY TRAITS:
Which of These Sound Most Like YOU?

What sort of a "personality" are you? In each of the following sets of traits, put a check beside the one that best describes you.

- ❑ I'm quiet and reserved.
- ❑ I'm talkative and outgoing.

- ❑ I like to be with a lot of people, even large groups or a crowd.
- ❑ I prefer to be alone or in small groups.
- ❑ I'm an "up-front and out-there" sort of person.
- ❑ I'm a "behind the scenes" sort of person.

- ❑ I'm a high-energy person.
- ❑ I'm laid-back.

- ❑ I love animals.
- ❑ I don't particularly like to be around animals.

- ❑ I much prefer indoor activities over outdoor activities.
- ❑ I prefer outdoor activities over indoor activities.

- ❑ I'm a good listener, sympathetic and compassionate to the needs of others.
- ❑ I'm not particularly interested in the trials and tribulations of people.

- ❑ I love working with people.
- ❑ I prefer reading, writing or working on my computer than working with people.

- ❑ I'm disciplined and a self-starter.
- ❑ I'm spontaneous and prefer just going with the flow.

- ❑ I love being a team player (doing things with others).
- ❑ I have an entrepreneurial spirit (I prefer to go it alone).

- ❑ In my spare time, I prefer to hang out in my room.
- ❑ In my spare time, I prefer to do things with others.

- ❑ When it comes to my leisure time, I prefer solitary, but physical, activities, such as rearranging the furniture in my room or riding a bicycle.

❑ When it comes to my leisure time, I prefer solitary and quiet activities, such as reading.

❑ When it comes to my leisure time, I prefer to be social and active, such as shooting hoops or playing miniature golf.
❑ When it comes to my leisure time, I prefer social but quiet activities, such as listening to music or going to the movies.

❑ When it comes to sports, I prefer to be a spectator.
❑ When it comes to sports, I prefer playing to watching.

❑ When it comes to clothes and my appearance, I prefer being casual more than being formal.
❑ When it comes to clothes and my appearance, I prefer being formal more than being casual.

❑ I like to write about things.
❑ I like to read about things.
❑ I prefer "doing" more than writing or reading.

❑ I like to be a leader giving others direction.
❑ I prefer taking directions and carrying out what needs to be done.
❑ I prefer to figure things out on my own.

❑ I like working with my hands, creating or repairing things.
❑ I'm an "idea person" who would rather design things in my head and on paper and leave production to someone else.
❑ I'm better with written instructions on how to do things.

❑ Given the choice, I'd prefer to study alone.
❑ Given the choice, I'd prefer to study in a group.

❑ I learn best by hearing.
❑ I learn best by reading.
❑ I learn best when I can see a visual, like a timeline or photos.

❑ For me to buy into something, I need facts and proof.
❑ I'm a spiritual person and find it easy to have faith in things; not all things need a concrete reason for being in order to have merit.

❑ I would consider it more fun to read a book about hiking up a mountain than to hike up a mountain.
❑ I would consider it more fun to hike up a mountain than to read a book about hiking up a mountain.

❑ I'm the friend who is most comfortable going along with what the group wants to do.

❑ I'm the friend who is making suggestions and decisions and telling the group how things are going to be.

❑ I have a funny bone; I look for the ironies and humor in a situation.

❑ I tend to be a serious person.

❑ I spend my money as soon as I get it.

❑ Saving money comes naturally to me.

❑ I most enjoy spending my money on "things to do" (concerts, dances, movies, horse-riding, going to the zoo).

❑ I most enjoy spending my money on "things to have" (clothes, skin and hair products).

❑ I most enjoy spending my money on "ways to be" (I'm naturally interested in self-improvement, such as being a better communicator, learning a second language, sharpening my intuition).

❑ I prefer to "seize the day" and live in the moment.

❑ I prefer to "think about tomorrow" and plan.

❑ When spending time with friends, I'm usually the one doing the most talking.

❑ When spending time with friends, I'm usually the one doing the most listening.

❑ When I hang out with friends, I prefer going to the movies or a concert.

❑ When I hang out with friends, I prefer sitting around sharing the latest news and ideas we each have.

❑ I prefer hanging around with just a few close friends than being in a large group of friends.

❑ I prefer hanging around with a big circle of friends as opposed to being with just a couple of friends.

❑ I'd prefer to be alone than spend time with others.

❑ What people think of me is important to me.

❑ I'm not as concerned about what other people think of me, if I'm comfortable with myself.

What Did You Learn About Yourself?

In thinking about your response the questions, what did you discover about yourself? Of course, there may be others that best describe your personality, but the point is to ask yourself what trends you see. For example, is it apparent that you prefer working in groups rather than spending time alone (or was the opposite true)? Do you prefer "machines" to people—or is the opposite true? Do you prefer spending time with animals more than time with people—or was the opposite true?

You may want to make a list of the trends that emerge from the profile. For example, you might say, "I'm social, like people, prefer group activities, like to be active, prefer being the group leader." And so on.

The goal is to be able to describe yourself as "I am a person who_____(and be able to answer the question).

Do this now. _____

_____

_____

_____

Our Personality is Always "On Display"

Our personality is evident to those around us. When you can, ask the following four individuals to give you three words that best describe you. Write down what they said.

My favorite teacher, said he/she would describe me as a person who:

_____

_____ .

My father (or stepfather) said he would describe me as a person who:

_____

_____ .

My mother (or stepmother) said she would describe me as a person who:

_____

_____ .

My best friend, said he/she would describe me as a person who:

_____

_____ .

Now think about how each has described you. Do you see any "trends"? For example, do their comments or description of you suggest that you're a "people-person," or a "behind-the-scenes organizer"? Do they describe you as "outgoing," "shy," or as a "private person"? Make a list of their comments, grouping together those that seem a lot alike.

The Traits That Make You, YOU

Understanding the traits that make you into the person you are is more than interesting information. Knowing your personality can help you set goals that are in sync with your identity. For example:

<u>Fitness</u>: "As a PE elective, should I take tennis or volleyball?"

<u>Social</u>: "Should I try out for the pep squad or take a photography course?"

<u>Learning</u>: "Should I sign up for one-on-one tutoring, or join a tutoring group?"

If you know that you enjoy group interaction more than solitary experiences, then naturally you'd sign up for being in activities where you'd be with others. If your personality preference is more of enjoying self, introspective or one-on-one experiences, then you would naturally choose activities accordingly.

Knowing your personality can also help you make choices about jobs or careers in which you feel you're best suited. Asking (and answering) questions such as, "Am I an 'up-front and out-there' sort of person, or a 'private, behind-the-scenes' sort of person" can then help you make choices such as:

- "Would I enjoy being a comedian?" or, "Do I have what it takes to be a private detective?"
- "Should I plan for working with animals?" or "Am I a 'mechanics and machines' sort of person?"
- "Do I need to be around other people in order to be most happy, creative and productive?"
- "In choosing the 'setting' for my work, would I prefer a job that allows me to be mostly outdoors or indoors?"
- "Would I prefer a job where I constantly travel to new places and am always meeting 'new faces,' or would something like that not suit me at all?"
- "Would I like to work for myself, and if so, would I prefer

to work from a home office where it's just me and my office, or work alone but in an office located in a busy downtown high-rise?"

Of course, lifestyle and job and career choices are something you'll get a chance to discover more about when you take courses such as career exploration. But if your goal is to make, as Jennifer says, "Your joys your jobs; your toys your tools," then knowing about your personality is important and useful information.

What other ways can you think of to use the information you've discovered about your personality to shape goals for your life, now and in the future?

_____

_____

Where can you go, or whom can you turn to, to learn more about and to explore your personality on a deeper, more formal level? For example:
- I could check with my school counselor.
- I could take a weekend course at a junior college near me.

If you have no idea, be sure to list who you could ask who would know your options for finding out this information.

You can use the new insights you've gained to direct you as you set goals. But personality is just one indicator of "who" you are; "aptitude" is another. Like our personality, our aptitudes reveal what comes easily (naturally) for us, and what doesn't.

In the next chapter, you'll learn about the nine very different aptitudes, and identify which ones are a "natural" for you, as well as which are not! You'll also get a chance to see how you can use them to shape goals.

Before you read the next chapter, take a moment to list what you feel are there of your aptitudes.

- _____

- _____

- _____

CHAPTER 5
Your Aptitudes: What Do You Do Best?

When I Finally Knew—"For Sure"

It was only the two of us, my friend and me, standing on the stage at a packed auditorium. All eyes were on us. While I relished this, friend was so nervous she said she felt as though she was going to "throw up."

My enjoyment of speaking in front of others began when I was a freshman when I took a child-development class at school. As part of our class work, we had to complete a certain number of hours doing volunteer work with children. I chose a day-care center assisting with the children's class assignments, as well as play-yard duty. I really enjoyed it. I thought it was a lot of fun. I find kids interesting; you never know what they might say or do, and they're just so cute!

One day the teacher talked about some of the work she used to do at Casa de Ampara, a center for abused, neglected and abandoned children. I couldn't help but think of how difficult it must be for children to be away from their parents, their home, their toys—even though it was in their best interests to have a safe place to live.

When our teacher asked us to get involved in community service, right away I knew I wanted to volunteer at Casa de Ampara.

Sometimes when I arrived at Casa and asked for my assignment for the day, they'd say, "Read to the kids," and sometimes it was "Play with the kids." Playing with the children, helping them to have fun, to laugh and learn games brought them happiness, and was good for their social development.

My time at Casa was a precious experience for me and so insightful. I found out a lot about how the "child protective system" works; I also found out about other programs that help children who are in foster homes for years. One of those programs was *Voices for Children*. One of the things this organization does is helps kids become eligible for adoption. I was shocked to see how many children who are "wards" of the courts.

Then, on September 11, 2001 America was attacked, and the World Trade Center was destroyed. When I learned that thousands had perished in this horrific terrorist attack, my first thoughts were about all the children in day-care centers whose parents wouldn't be coming to get them that day. I just hurt for them and I wanted to do something to help. But what? I couldn't go to them, since I was on the other side of the country, but I could find a way to raise money to send to them. But how? Who would I get to help?

Then I remembered that in a few weeks there would be a community meeting scheduled in the school auditorium. All the area business owners would be there, and a huge community picnic would take place. That took care of the when and where! As for who would help me, the most likely candidates seemed to be my friends; maybe it could be a project for my civics class and the kids in my church youth group, too. Finally, I needed to figure out the how. It had to be minimal cost, maximum profit. I couldn't get clear on the one perfect thing— was it a product or a service?

For the next few days, my "cause" was all I could think about. As I drove to school, I noticed all the flags and patriotic signs that had gone up all over town. They were on the freeway over-passes, in front of houses and businesses, even on our school's scoreboards and bulletin boards. An idea began to formulate, and by the time I pitched my fund-raising goal to my civics class: "We can sell something patriotic—something red, white and blue."

"Like pins or flags?" someone asked. "How about ribbons?" and it all took off from there. We took up a collection at school and within our community and collected enough money to buy red, white and blue ribbons and some nice stickpins. Then I put together a production committee, and we made these simple looped red, white and blue pins—five hundred of them—for a few pennies each. I got together another committee with some of the best artists and computer masters on our school campus. We created flyers and got out the word of our cause and where we'd be fund-raising on the day of the picnic.

I set up shifts to cover our booth at the picnic. We set up a table outside so that everyone coming into the auditorium would first have to pass by our "Ribbons for the Children" sales table. When the event was over, especially after my on-stage pitch, we made over nine hundred dollars, since a whole lot of people donated even more than the one dollar we were asking.

The money was sent to the Red Cross, earmarked for the children who had lost parents that fateful day. After the event was over, I felt both happy and satisfied how it had all come together. I also realized that I am most happy when I was organizing things and leading the way to make them happen.

I guess that was the moment I knew for sure what I'd like to do with my "natural ability." I thrive on organizing others toward a goal. I find it easy to do. This has made me think that I'd like to get a degree in an area that would help me get a job with an organization such as the United Way, or even fundraising, something that allows me to make the lives of kids better.

So that's where I'm at right now, finding out what degree would best help me do what I'd like to do. I'm also looking into organizations, such as the United Way, and trying to find out more about what they do. And I've already asked the senior fundraiser for Casa de Ampara if I can spend "Shadow Day"—where you get to spend a day with a professional in the community—with her (she said yes!). So that's what I'm up to now. —**Sara Knorr, 18**

What Are Your "Strong Points"—What Do You Know "For Sure"?

Sara Knorr has a special knack for organizing others in meeting a common goal, especially when tied with her great interest in helping children. She put two and two together and realized that this was special and important to her, and that she could make things happen. Along the way, Sara also discovered what she wants to do for a career.

Finding those things for which you have a natural curiosity and attraction is important information in letting your natural abilities shine. Have you had an experience, like Sara, that made you realize you had a certain passion for what it was you were doing or involved in?

DISCOVERING YOUR "STRENGTHS"

Our strengths—the areas in which we learn most easily—are different for most of us. Perhaps your friend has a talent for picking up the latest dance steps within moments of being shown, while you must really work at it and, even then, find yourself talking your way through the latest move. Another friend seems to have a real talent for remembering things she sees but is not so good at remembering things she hears. Perhaps you, like Thomas Hatfield, have a natural ability to work with the computer, even finding the idea of creating 3-D animation to be a snap, while your best friend is still fearful to use a computer for fear she'll touch a key that will "crash the hard drive and everything on the computer will be lost." What accounts for such disproportionate differences in our abilities? It's because we each have different aptitudes. Harvard psychologist Howard Gardner has discovered at least nine different and distinct types of intelligence. His research suggests that we are "good" at only a few of these—which means that we are not so good (and in varying degrees) at the others.

This is useful information. Not only does it confirm why some things are easy for us while others are more difficult, but such information can steer us in the direction of setting and achieving goals accordingly. What are your strengths? Of the nine aptitudes, which ones come easily for you, and which are the most difficult for you to master?

The following can help you find out.

The 9 Types of Intelligence—Our Aptitudes

As you read each one of the nine types of Intelligence, think about which your strongest point is, then the second best, and then your third and so on, all the way through to nine being the least easy for you. When you are done reading all nine, come back and number them, from your strongest (1) to the weakest (9).

_____ **Verbal or Linguistic Intelligence**. This is your ability to read and write, to use words well. Writers, speakers and politicians develop this type of intelligence. People who are linguistically intelligent are systematic, enjoying patterns and order, which is why they enjoy word games and have a good memory for trivia. This is the teen who gets voted in as a class officer, writes for the school paper, turns in terrific term papers and remembers jokes—even those knock-knock jokes from elementary years!

_____ **Logical or Mathematical Intelligence**. This is your ability to reason or calculate. People who have well-developed logical intelligence like to count and be precise, such as scientists, mathematicians and lawyers. They are good at deductive thinking, using computers and problem-solving, and like the orderly basis of programming and application. This is the teen who enjoys his math classes, keeps his room and closet organized, and will remember that your borrowing something from him, and when!

_____ **Musical or Rhythmic Intelligence**. We often classify musical ability as a "gift," when in fact it is an aptitude, an intelligence. Musically intelligent people are very sensitive to the emotional power of music and find it easy to learn dates and other "have-to-memorize" material, most especially if it is set to rhythm, like poetry or rap. They like to use music to relax, to change their moods and are said to be deeply spiritual. Composers, conductors and musicians are obviously strong in musical intelligence, as are clergymen and spiritual healers, and those teens who are in their school band, play an instrument—or have formed or play in a band of their own!

_____ Spatial or Visual Intelligence. People with this intelligence can remember things well when they are put into picture form; they can memorize maps and charts. They like to see the whole picture all at once, rather than learning in bits and pieces. They use mental images and metaphors for learning. Architects, sculptors and pilots test high in this area, as do those teens who love classes in which they can express creativity. They are always doodling on their notebooks or drawing "pictures" or symbols on their notes—whether it be class notes or notes to friends or "someone special."

_____ Kinesthetic or Physical Intelligence. This is highly developed in athletes, dancers, gymnasts, and surgeons. Kinesthetically intelligent people have good control over their bodies and like to participate in sports, dance, and anything that requires movement. They have good timing and are highly sensitive to the physical environment. These are people who learn best by doing, touching or moving objects around. Professional athletes would be identified as those having "kinesthetic" intelligence, as well as the teen who is consistently on a sports team in his or her school or community.

_____ Interpersonal or People Intelligence. A "people-person" relates well to others and understands the feelings of others. This is the teen who loves to join groups, is very social, a good communicator and does well in activities that require partners or teamwork. Salespeople, negotiators, motivational speakers and coaches are good examples of those high in interpersonal skills—as are those teens who are identified as "talkative" or "very social."

_____ Intrapersonal or Intuitive Intelligence. This intelligence is often called intuition. It is the ability to tap into information stored in the subconscious mind. Psychologists, hypnotherapists, mystics and counselors show this type of intelligence. People who have intrapersonal intelligence are extremely interested in understanding the motives of people (what makes people tick), including themselves. They are sensitive toward their own feelings, as well as the feelings of others. They are especially in touch with their own feelings and are said to be "reserved" although they readily intuit (understand) what they learn and how it relates to others. They don't like to conform; they like to be independent and take control of their own learning. This is the person who others come to when they have a broken heart or are uncertain, even confused, about their feelings.

_____ **Naturalist or Nature Intelligence**. A "nature" person loves the outdoors, animals and those things having to do with nature. This person is "in tune" with nature and is not likely to be afraid of spiders or other "creatures." He or she is likely to have a pet, whether it be a dog, cat, fish or reptile, and would prefer reading a book on the adventure of an animal as opposed to the adventure of a person. A volcanist (someone who studies volcanoes) exhibits nature intelligence, as does someone who saves a lizard, bird or mouse from the jaws of his or her cat.

_____ **Philosophical or Existentialist Intelligence**. People of this intelligence ponder life in relationship to the "bigger picture" such as demonstrating concern about the well-being of the planet, the world or the "world's citizens," or those who find meaning in being of service to humanity. Leaders, whether a president of a country, a "Mother Teresa" within a community, or a religious or spiritual leader all qualify as having philosophical intelligence. The teen who leads a school or community drive to make the world a better place or who concerns himself with saving the rainforest or seeking his and others' "spiritual journey" also demonstrates this type of intelligence.

Focus on Your Strengths; Shore up Weaker Areas

Again, no one of these nine is better to "be" than the others. All are good; all show you areas of talent and aptitude (or lack thereof). This information can help point you in the direction of a job or career for which you may be well-suited. For example, if you love to play both the guitar and the flute and learning to play them "came naturally" to you, perhaps the field of music will be fun for you. Having a talent for reading maps and drawing them to scale could mean that a career in the field of architecture and so on.

You can also use this information to stop fretting about things you seen not to "get the hang of." For example, if you are not at all musically inclined, you may not want to take the time to learn a musical instrument. Sara Knorr has compassion for children and a knack for organizing others in getting things done. Sara may want to consider getting a degree in personnel management or fundraising and so on. You can even use this information to set goals for turning a "weak area" into something you want to make stronger.

To give you an idea how you can use information about your aptitudes to set goals, we asked Sara Knorr to list her first, second and third strengths and tell us why she chose as she did. Here is her response:

#1   Interpersonal or People Intelligence: I chose this one first because I'm a "people-person." I know that I relate well to others and understand their feelings. I love group activities (in fact, I love to start groups—and already started two at my school and one at my church). I'm very social, a good communicator, and I do great in activities that require partners or teamwork. Since salespeople, motivational speakers and coaches are good examples of those high in interpersonal skills, and I know that I'm good at selling others on my ideas and motivating them to take up my cause—as well as at coaching them through it—this must be my strongest area.

#2   Linguistic Intelligence: I chose this area next because everyone agrees I can be very persuasive with words—both in letter-writing and when making speeches. I'm very systematic; I enjoy having a goal, and then seeing that it's met. And I'm a person who likes order. I can see that in my room—I like it neat and orderly. Even my closet is organized.

#3   Intrapersonal or Intuitive Intelligence: I'd say I'm not as strong in this area as the other two, but I chose it because I feel I'm intuitive (and I hope sensitive, although I can be impatient when things aren't getting done according to plan). I'm also self-motivated. I'm aware of my strengths, like being able to organize others.

Next, we asked Sara how she might use knowing about her strengths and weaknesses in setting goals. Here is what she said:

"Learning about the nine areas is useful for me in several ways. For example, I know for sure now that getting a degree in organizational and leadership skills. My strongest area is in Interpersonal or People Intelligence, so I believe I'd be good at motivating and directing others to take action. I could be a social service agency's Public Relations specialist or fundraiser. I could train and manage staff or do community outreach campaigns. (I'd choose to work for a program that helps children.)

Since I also have Linguistic Intelligence, I could put my "way with words" to use in any of those jobs! Since I love to create order, I'd also be great as a program coordinator or director. And now that I can see that I'm not as sensitive to people's feelings as I thought I was, I want to get better at that."

Now try this for yourself. List your first, second and third strengths, and explain why you chose them, and how you can use this information to be deliberate in setting goals.

#1 _____

_____

I chose this because: _____

#2 _____

_____

I chose this because: _____

#3 _____

_____

I chose this because: _____

What Do Others See As Your Talents, Strengths and Aptitudes?

Our strengths are often obvious to others. Ask three people whose opinion you trust what it is they think that your talents, strengths and aptitudes are, and why they think so.

Are there any similarities to what they say? For example, do their comments reflect that you are good with people, or that you are best at getting things done on your own? Do they perceive you as being a stick-to-the-facts kind of person or do they see you as more of a creative "visionary" who stimulates ideas and sees things from a multifaceted point of view? Make a list of what others say about your aptitudes and think about how you can best use this information to set goals.

Knowing your aptitudes is a powerful way to acknowledge and appreciate who you are. Another way to better know yourself lies in understanding how our hobbies show us a slice of "who we are." What are your hobbies and how can you use them to set goals for yourself? The next chapter will shed light on what's true for you!

CHAPTER 6

Your Hobbies: Setting Goals That Explore Your "Innate" Interests

"All Dolled Up"

I was ready to meet my new date! I was looking "hot" or as my grandpa likes to say whenever my sister, Elise, and I get dressed up, "all dolled up."

Our grandfather lives with us, and we adore him. He's sweet, funny and just fun to be around. He teases us and we tease him—especially whenever he uses his ancient expressions, such as "all dolled up." We think "all dolled up" sounds funny, so we laugh and tell him thank you. Then whenever he puts on what he calls his "Sunday finest," we tell him he looks "hot"—but he doesn't get it, so we just say, "You look 'all dolled up,'" and he just laughs.

But funny thing about that saying of his, I'm now actually thinking of making "All Dolled Up" the name of my own business!

Ever since I was a little girl, I've had this thing about dolls. I mean, Elise did, too, but she didn't go to the extreme that I did. I considered my dolls special and kept them in perfect shape. Hers would become ratty over the months of wear and tear and always lost their tiny shoes hats and hair accessories. Most of her dolls even ended up with missing limbs! Not mine. Even Elise commented that my dolls seemed to look better the longer I owned them. I'd make them little clothes and keep them immaculate. If they had hair, they ended up changing hairstyles as often as I did.

Eventually, Elisa went through a stage of loving fish, then horses, and now, she's into boys! Dolls are not for my sister anymore. This is not the case for me; I've never lost interest in my now vast collection of dolls. I went on to makeup and boys and a part-time job at a department store, but I kept my prized doll collection and I've added more and more to it over the years.

I also began buying antique and collectible dolls. Some of them are complete wrecks, but I've found I have a very special knack for restoring them to picture perfection. I go to garage sales to see if I can find old dolls to buy and restore them to good condition if they need it.

If I eventually feel the doll isn't one I wish to keep I sell it. I've made more money off my hobby than I have from any part-time job. And sometimes I donate a doll to a charity where they can sell the doll for a great deal of money. I even belong to an organization for doll collectors, and I get a monthly magazine. Once I sent in an article for consideration, and it was published. That was a few months back and now the magazine has offered me a regular column and they will even pay me for it!

In a few months I start college, where I'm going to take business courses so I can learn how to run a successful business, like a collector's doll shop, complete with departments for appraisal, restoration, and purchase and trading. If you happen to see a sign on a shop that reads "All Dolled Up," stop on in and check out my store! —Shana Nixon, 17

What a Hobby Reveals About You

It's obvious that Shana loves her hobby of collecting and restoring dolls so much so that she loses all track of time while working on them. She plans on getting a college education centered on turning her hobby into a career. Hobbies are like that. Not only do they reveal what you find interesting, but they also shed light on who you are.

Maybe you have a friend who collects stamps from various states and countries while another friend has a "green thumb" who is interested in growing flowers, even "splicing" them to see if she can produce a hybrid plant from combining two from the same species.

While you may think of your hobbies as "just for fun," a closer look can help you uncover another facet of "who you are," revealing your true nature for what you find interesting and rewarding to do for work, such as a job or career. Again, all of it is useful information as you set about creating goals to bring you happiness, satisfaction and fulfillment.

Here are five good reasons to discover and develop a hobby.

5 Reasons to Discover and Develop Your Hobbies

1. <u>A hobby allows you to refine skills and develop new ones</u>. We asked Shana what skills she develops while engaged in her hobby. "I developed patience because I have to concentrate while paying attention to all the detail involved in repairing cracks and painting on faces, and I use negotiation skills when I buy and sell my dolls. I also do a great deal of research in learning about the market values for different dolls."

2. <u>Some hobbies allow time alone—time to be with yourself</u>. Even if your hobby includes interacting with others (such as trading sports cards), it still allows you private peaceful moments with yourself. Shana's sister, Elise, while she wasn't interested in dolls, found a hobby when her grandmother gave me an amaryllis plant. "There was something about that amaryllis that intrigued me," she said. The instructions for caring for the plant explained that under just the right conditions, the plant would bloom twice a year rather than just the usual once. I decided I was going to coax the plant to bloom twice that year, Elise said, and it did. I started adding some other kinds of amaryllis plants, and one thing lead to another. My goal now is to have a small greenhouse to experiment with other plants. I just love the unhurried alone time, and I'm intrigued with nature's plants and growth cycles.

3. <u>A hobby allows you to discover things about yourself that you might never learn otherwise</u>. Hobbies give you those moments to get in touch with that part of yourself that wouldn't get expression otherwise. Elise said her hobby taught her she loves to nurture things and watch them grow, something she never would've known about herself if she hadn't been given that first amaryllis. Shana, on the other hand, likes to restore things to their original perfection. "Hobbies are so diverse," Shana added. "My boyfriend's hobby is cycling. Not only does he ride, but he also rebuilds bicycles, something he says taught him that he's creative—a word that he never would've used before to describe himself."

4. <u>A hobby allows you to set your own "standards of excellence</u>." So much in our culture coaches us to compete and compare ourselves with others. This isn't the case with a hobby; you get to excel to the level of your own choosing; you don't have to be better than someone else, nor are you held back to the level of another person. In your hobby, you are your own Einstein. As Elise reported, she doesn't feel any pressure; she just works on her amaryllis hobby for her own satisfaction—trying for extra blooms and experimenting with creating cross-breeds only for her own sense of achievement.

5. <u>Hobbies can reveal your true nature for work or a career</u>. Looking closely at what brings you great satisfaction can help you discover your talents, passions and aptitudes. We've seen how this worked for Shana, who has decided to make her hobby her life's work, but sometimes the direction your hobby gives you can be much more subtle. Elise, for example, doesn't want to raise amaryllis plants for a

living—she wants to go to college to become a preschool teacher. Yet in that work she'll still can nurture and watch the children grow.

Many plastic surgeons are drawn to is sculpting or painting, whereas race-car drivers, with their desire for speed have hobbies like bungee jumping or parachuting.

While you may not make your hobby your life's work, listen to what it is telling you about your true nature for work; it may be pointing you in the direction of "making your joys your job, your toys your tools."

Do you have a hobby? If you do, and even if you don't, what could it say about you? The following can help you find out.

What are Your Hobbies?

Here are a series of questions to get you thinking about the importance of hobbies as to how they may lead you to know more about yourself.

- How would you define a hobby?
- Why do you think having a hobby is a good thing?
- Do you have a hobby? If so, what is it? How long have you had this hobby? What is it that you most enjoy about this hobby?
- If you do not have a hobby, what hobby would you like to investigate most?
- Do you have more than one hobby? If so, what are the others?
- Does anyone you know have more than one hobby?
- Is this hobby something that you do alone, or are others involved in it? For example, is it a team sport, or are you cycling alone?
- Does your hobby require that you interact with others? For example, are you sharing information while trading baseball cards, or are you working quiety on a woodworking project?
- Does the fact that you're alone or interacting with others play a part in your attraction to this hobby?
- If you don't already have a hobby, do you feel you would be more drawn to hobbies that involve interaction, or hobbies that you'd do alone?
- What achievements, awards or recognition have you received as a result of your hobby?
- What skills are associated with your hobby? For example, Shana listed: concentration, researching, negotiating, problem-solving and creativity. (If you don't have a hobby, pick one that you'd like to learn more about and make a list of the skills you

think it would help you to develop.)
- Do you have a hobby that allows you to experiment or explore? How does it do this? How does experimenting help you set goals?
- What arts and crafts do you make? What do you collect?
- What skills are related to your hobby? For example; having self-discipline or being a team player.

Talk to Others About How They Discovered Their Hobby

What can you learn in watching how others have turned their hobbies into something more than leisure-time activities? Talk to someone who has made his hobby also his work. This could be someone such as the baseball card shop owner if you collect baseball cards, a professional ball player if your hobby is softball or an artisan if you're into crafts. Ask him or her all about it. How did this person get started? What career opportunities does the hobby hold? Has it helped this person with goals he or she had in developing relationships? What about with developing goals in education? Learn from your "hobby expert."

What, if Any, Financial Goals Do You Need To Set for Your Hobby?

Do you need to make ten dollars a month or seventy-five dollars a month to keep up your hobby? If so, how will you earn that money?

_____

_____

What goal would you like to set that can help you discover or develop your hobby?_____

_____

What other ways can you think of to use the information you've discovered about your hobby to shape goals for your life, now and in the future? _____

_____

Maybe you think you don't have a hobby or any interest that could lead to one, but there are ways to find guidance in selecting a hobby. Think about those times when something you're doing captures your attention to the point that you lose all sense of time. At those times, what are you doing?

If You Don't Have a Hobby, Do You Think That's a Negative?

Where can you go, or whom can you turn to, to learn more about your hobby? For example, does your school counselor have books or resources that can help you? Be sure to ask! Think of all the places you could go to gather more information. Example: I could take a weekend course at a junior college near me.

_____

_____

_____

_____

As you can see, a hobby can play a big role in getting to know ourselves. Feeling that we know ourselves, liking the "face in the mirror," is the basis of a positive, and authentic, self-esteem.

CHAPTER 7

What Do You Want to Achieve Today, Tomorrow and in the Future?

Thinking Big (Enough)

The previous information focused on discovering "who" you are. This chapter will focus on the "what" you want. The goal is to "think big" as you explore goals to set for yourself. Each complements the other: "Knowing yourself" allows you to set goals that you will use and further develop your interests, talents and strengths.

Setting and achieving goals that are "totally you" helps you to feel in touch with yourself, happy, hopeful and fulfilled. What "mechanism" do you use to think about all you want out of life? For example, do you:

- pal around with interesting and creative friends because being with them stimulates you to "think big"?
- read broadly, exposing yourself to great minds because it expands your own sense of things?
- attend classes and seminars to "stimulate" your thinking?
- watch TV shows and films that are interesting and educational?
- observe others evaluating if their lifestyle is one you'd like to emulate?

Do You Have a "Dream Machine"?

Have you thought about what you want out of life, both now for the coming days and weeks, and for the months, even years, ahead? Do you have a "dream machine"? How does knowing what you want help you feel in charge? Here's how 16-year-old Brandon White answered the question.

"Cool, Yet a Little Overwhelming, Too"

"On some days I feel really in control, which is a feeling I like. I especially feel 'in charge' at times like when I've prepared for my classes and it really paid off or when I'm called on in class and I can answer a question intelligently. I feel 'in charge' when I get to use the family car and drive myself to and from school.

I feel 'in charge' when I've just deposited a portion of my paycheck from my part-time job into my savings account to go toward buying a car, going to college and other things. But there are also times when I'm just glad that I'm living with my parents and all I have to do is focus on doing well for the day at hand, like when I'm comparing car insurance or looking over the tuition and fees to get into a college and thinking I'll be in debt forever. I'd have to say that while I'm feeling 'in charge' most of the time, at other times I'm happy to know I still have a little time before I must be completely responsible for all the decisions that I know are mine to eventually make. But I do have big plans for myself, because I want to be a success in my life." —Brandon White, 16

How about you? Whether you are at the stage of having wishes but not yet having turned them into goals, or whether you're able to identify an entire list of things you'd like to accomplish, either way, it's good you're revving up your "go for it" battery.

How Do You Define Success?

"When I got arrested for being under the influence of alcohol at a concert," Lyle said, *"I thought it was the worst thing that could ever happen to me. But now I can see I wasn't only arrested; I was actually rescued."*

Lyle was court-ordered into an alcohol awareness program where he learned about alcoholism, about himself and about how to live a life of sobriety. *"I learned so much. One day at a time, I know I can live a successful life sober. Now, there are so many things I want to achieve. One of my most important goals is to become an alcohol awareness educator teaching DUI classes,"* Lyle explains. *"While I never ended up with a DUI, I know that's where I was headed, and I'd like to help others who weren't as lucky as I was. I know firsthand how helpless and desperate being addicted to alcohol can make you feel, and I know firsthand that there's a way out."*

With more than two years of sobriety, Lyle is now enrolled in college where he's completing courses to become certified as an alcohol and drug counselor. He volunteers at the outpatient program that he was once court-ordered to attend and has an intern- ship at a "teen recovery center" in his area. *"Right now, success means two things to me: continuing to stay sober one day at a time (that's the biggest one), and two, to have a full-time career as an alcohol awareness educator."* Already quite a success in his recovery, Lyle is well on his way to achieving his new goals.

What Makes a Person Successful?

Would you say that Lyle Rincon, who overcame alcoholism and was then moved to create a career of helping others around his experience, was a success?

What one person sees as success is not always the same as what the next person perceives it to be. To some, being a success may mean making a lot of money, while to another it may be winning a tough competition, and to yet another it could be overcoming a seemingly insurmountable obstacle. To someone else "being successful" may be seen as having attained material things such as a fancy car, a "dream home" or owning nicely tailored clothes, while for another it's having earned the recognition, admiration and love of friends and family. For still others, it may be "peace of mind" or being healthy and feeling energetic and able to do the things the person wants to do. Success might even be perceived as an achievement, such as having lowered a sprint time, raised a math score, earned a college diploma or secured a position.

You can define success in many ways. Do you wonder why defining success is important? Knowing what you consider the mark of success for you helps you set your goals to reach that success.

Lyle Rincon's definition of success is to help others understand and overcome alcoholism. Knowing this, Lyle has a direction for setting goals to secure a career in that field. Defining success helps you figure out where it is you want to go so that you can then set goals to get you there. Answering the following questions can help you explore your definition of success.

- Who is the most successful person you know, and why would you say this person is a success? _____

  _____

  _____

- Name a success you have had in the last month. What goals did you set for achieving it?_____

  _____

  _____

- Take a moment to think about your three biggest successes in life to date. What are they? Describe each one.

  1. _____

     _____

  2. _____

     _____

  3. _____

     _____

- What do these "successes" tell you about your definition of "success"? _____

  _____

  _____

- How will being "successful" make you different from how you are now? In what ways will you be different? _____

  _____

  _____

- What one thing would you like to do or learn but haven't yet tried? What keeps (or prevents) you from accomplishing this?

  _____

  _____

As you can see, your definition of success is all your own. It's important in that it becomes your "blueprint" for setting those goals that will get you from here to there. Whether you're building a birdhouse or a castle, it will be helpful to have the right set of blueprints, the right goals. Speaking of castles, have you ever wondered if you are dreaming big enough? The next chapter will help you see if you are!

CHAPTER 8

Are You Dreaming "Big Enough"?

Are You Afraid to Be ". . . Gorgeous, Talented, Fabulous"?

I really wanted to run for class office at my school. Winning would be so great—but losing, well, if I didn't win, I'd be the "loser." I went back and forth between "go for it" and "don't do it," wondering what to do. Then, in the middle of trying to get beyond my "fear of losing," I saw a poster with the words of author Marianne Williamson, where she makes the point that "our deepest fear is not that we are inadequate" . . . but rather, "our deepest fear is that we are powerful beyond measure." She believes that people say they want to be "gorgeous, talented and fabulous," but they're afraid to be. Yet we have every right to those qualities since, she says, we are "a child of God" and "playing small doesn't serve the world." In other words, letting your light shine is what you're supposed to do. Her words stopped the battle going on in my head; I decided right then and there to "Go for it!" But her words also made me think about whether I had really been afraid of losing—or afraid that I might win! Was I afraid I'd be in the position of having to save face, or showing my face (leading)? As I was searching for an answer to my question, I remembered her advice to "let your light shine" and that, in doing that, we give others the "permission to do the same." That poster made me a fan of Marianne Williamson that day—and a campaigner for the office of class president! —**Corey Richards, 17**

Your "Dream Machine": Don't Leave Home Without It

Corey isn't alone in his admiration for Marianne's words. We agree wholeheartedly with Corey's enthusiasm over Marianne Williamson's beautiful words, which come from her book, *A Return to Love*. It's reported that the great visionary, Nelson Mandela, was so taken by Marianne Williamson's point in our not playing "small" that he used her words in his message to the world following his inauguration as president of South Africa. Looking at his life, one can see how he embodied that message: Having been imprisoned for decades for his stand against apartheid, he was released to become the first black president of the very nation that had imprisoned him! Marianne's words became his dream—a grand and glorious vision he aspired to in his ongoing fight for human rights for his people and his country—one he realized only because he refused to "play small" and dared to dream big!

What about you? Is your desire to be "brilliant, gorgeous, talented and fabulous"? How will you ensure that you don't "play small," "shrink," or "feel insecure"? What are your plans so that you "manifest all that is within" and "let your own light shine"? How will you become "powerful beyond measure"? Aside from believing that all is possible, you'll need to set goals to live your life accordingly.

What is Your "Vision?"

Having a vision for what you want, your ideal and where you're headed is an important part of making a dream come true. Perhaps you have a pretty good idea about what you'd like to accomplish this week, this month or in the coming semester. Maybe you've even got things pretty much figured out for the coming year. But what about for your future?

The future always seems so far away, but it's not really. Consider the quote, "Nothing is so far away as yesterday." The truth is, your future begins again every moment. Get in the habit of thinking about your future as tomorrow—and not some nebulous date in the way-off land of years and years from now. Is your dream machine busy working on the dreams you want to accomplish for your future? It should be.

When you see your future, what do you see? It's helpful to create a vision in your mind's eye of your future.

CREATING A VISION FOR YOUR "FUTURE LIFE"

For each of the groups of questions below, picture yourself at twenty-five years of age. At the end of each question, ask yourself: "What goals did I have to meet to get here?" The goal is to help you think about things you want, and how you want them. The first part of all of that, is to dream big!

"My "Future" Life
- Where are you living—in what city and state? Are you renting an apartment, or buying a condo or house? What does your home look like? How big is it? Is it small or large? Is it one bedroom, two or three? What is the color of your carpet—or do you have stone or wood flooring? Describe your furniture, the pictures on the walls and your furnishings.

- What sort of car are you driving? What is the year, make and model? Did you buy your car or are you leasing it?

- What are you doing for work? Did you graduate from college and are you in your first job? Did you go to trade school and been in the workforce for a couple of years? Are you working for a company (large or small?) or for yourself? Are you paid by the hour or do you have a salary? How much do you earn a year?

- Do you have a savings account, checking account and credit cards? Are you working toward an even greater degree in education? What kind of classes are you taking for personal enrichment? How do you see yourself learning and growing—in what areas do you continue to study?

- Who are your friends? Are they the same faces from junior high and high school, or are they mostly new friends you've made at work and in your personal life, like working out at the gym, shopping and in your leisure-time activities?

- What kind of organizations or associations do you belong to? Are you involved in a club, business organization or church group? What memberships do you hold? Are you an officer or aspiring to an office in any of these affiliations?

- Do you work out regularly? Do you belong to your local gym or workout center? How often do you work out? Are you in good shape? Are your friends into fitness? What kind of activities are you involved in to stay fit?

- Do you enjoy cooking at home, or do you eat out as often as you can? What sorts of restaurants do you go to? Do you often have friends over for meals? Do they join you in the kitchen and help you cook the meal, or do you have the meal prepared ahead of time?

- How do you spend your weekends? What do you do for fun? Do you go fishing or hiking? Do you go to movies? Is the beach the place you'd like to relax, or do you prefer the pool? How often do you go on vacation, and how is your vacation spent?

- What are your hobbies? How often do you find the time to enjoy your hobby? Has your hobby also become something you do for work?

- Do you live alone or with a roommate? If you live with someone, how did you meet? What sort of person is he or she? What does he or she look like? What sort of a job does he or she have? Did that person graduate from college? Do the two of you share the same values? Do you have the same friends? Do you work out together and socialize together? Do you have pets?

- Are you single, dating, engaged or married? Describe the person you are dating (or married to). What does he or she look like? What sort of a job does he or she have? Did that person graduate from college? Do you already have kids? If not, do the two of you plan to have children and, if so, how many? Do you plan to send them to a public school, a private school, or homeschool them?

- What do you do for spiritual fulfillment? Do you set aside a regular time to pray or meditate? Do you read spiritual or inspirational literature? Do you belong to one church, or go to various churches? Are you practicing the faith you practiced when living with your parents?

When you want to believe in something, you also have to believe in everything that's necessary for believing in it!

Thinking about your future now allows you to plan for it, to "make it happen," which is what setting goals is all about.

Again, your dreams are those visions of success that pull you forward as you meet your goals. But even great dreamers need more than imagination to achieve their goals. They also need to believe in their dreams—as well as take responsibility for being "in charge" of completing whatever action is necessary to make those dreams come true. As Ugo Betti's great quote suggests, *"When you want to believe in something, you also have to believe in everything that's necessary for believing in it!"*

Are you ready and willing to be in charge? The next chapter will help you decide!

CHAPTER 9

Are You Willing to Be in Charge of Your Life?

I Am, I Can, I Will
I AM—two small words, and yet,
It's a powerful "place" in which to be.
It's my life, and I'm living it,
I am everything you see.

I am responsible for my actions,
And all the things I say and do.
I am responsible for my behavior,
And how I interact with you.

I am responsible for the level of my work,
And the choices that I make.
I am responsible for the values I profess,
And for the ways that I communicate.

I CAN—two small words, and yet,
It's a powerful "place" in which to be.
It's my life, and I'm living it,
Traveling the land, sky and sea.

I can earn the respect of others,
And gain their friendship true.
I can honor all things living, and
Take care of my mind, health and body, too.

I can do my best each day,
And I can know my best is great.
I can continue to progress,
And move closer to my fate.

I WILL—two small words, and yet,
It's a powerful "place" in which to be.
It's my life, and I'm living it,
I will be everything, just wait and see.

I will use my talents wisely,
Learn to manage the moods of life.
I will respect my ups and downs,
Ask for help in overcoming strife.

"I will" is a promise to see clearly;
It reveals my strength to win,
As I arrive at mutual resolutions,
And look for my answers from within.

I'm young, still learning, growing, changing,
Yet I have ideals, noble goals and plans,
For things like a healthy environment,
World peace and a crime-free land.
No longer a child, yet not an adult, I am a teenager still.
But don't underestimate my value,
Because I am, I can, and I will. — **Jennifer Leigh**

You are, as Jennifer so aptly states in her poem, "still learning, growing, changing," yet you are well on your way to becoming an adult. Naturally, this means that very soon you're going to have more say in the things you do and in the choices you make.

Are You Taking Responsibility for Your Life?

Having more control of your life means more than just lifestyle choices—such as staying up later or spending even more time with your friends. It means that almost everything is up to you: You are responsible for your health and well-being, for planning the events of your days and seeing things through to completion, for planning your future and doing those things that will bring about your goals and desires. In short, growing up is about taking responsibility for you.

Taking responsibility means that you can read the previous poem and say, "Me, too." It means thinking of yourself as being the architect of your own life. You design the plans, draw up the blueprints and oversee the construction. Of course, you don't do all the construction yourself. Your parents, family, teachers and others help "build" you; obviously, their influence helps shape the person you will become. But in the final analysis, what happens is up to you. Others will help, but it is your plan, your dream to be built.

Are you managing your life? Are YOU shaping the direction of your life? Or, are you letting others do it? The following section will give some clarity on how you feel about this.

TAKING CHARGE (OF YOUR LIFE)

Here are a set of questions designed to help you see if you are willing to take charge of planning for your life and how you envision it.

- How do you feel about your life right now? Are you "happy" with it, or is there something you would like to change?

  _____

  _____

- Would you say that your life is relatively exciting, or would you describe it as dull, boring, routine? Explain. If you feel like your life needs change in this area, what could you do to change it?

  _____

  _____

- Would you say that you are in control of your life, or do you feel like others have more say in the things that happen to you than you do?

  _____

  _____

- List two areas of your life in which you feel you have total control and explain how this is so. What's your part in owning this control?

  _____

  _____

- List two areas of your life in which you feel you have little or no control and explain why you know this is so. What, if anything, could you do to take charge in these areas—or are they better left to the care of others?

  _____

  _____

- Would you say that you're a person who sets goals, or that you let things happen randomly?

  _____

  _____

- Has the fear of failure or being criticized ever affected your ability to set and achieve goals?

  _____

  _____

- How can having a plan of action give you more control over all areas of your life?

  _____

  _____

- Would you say that you know yourself pretty well? Explain how this knowledge or lack of it can help you take responsibility for your life and your goals.

  _____

  _____

Feeling like you're "in charge" of your life is a terrific feeling. When you're ready and willing to take responsibility for creating success and living your dreams, you are in the perfect place to set those goals and implement the right plan of action to assure that you achieve them.

You'll Need a "Plan," a Road Map, to Accomplish Your Goals

Considering your interests, talents and aptitudes, combined with having created a vision of your future, you now have a good starting point for setting goals you'll find stimulating, exciting and worth achieving. This is true for going after the things you want now, such as good friends, good grades, playing sports, a great family life and time for yourself, as well as for what you want soon, such as going to college, getting a job and living on your own. Shaping the direction of your life is not only inspiring, but also motivating! And like we said, so much of it is up to you!

Remember, though, that what you do and the goals you put in place right now connect you to your future, so don't wait to get started on creating your dreams. Start now. Just as attending practice on a regular basis on the sports field equates to improved performance come game day, and consistently working for good grades each year equates to a better chance to graduate with good marks, setting goals and having a plan to achieve them is the surest path to being successful in bringing about the life you want.

> **Having a plan for achieving your goals
> is as important as the goals themselves**

Maybe you want to buy a used car, pass a test, save for college, get your parents to agree on a longer curfew, or maybe you have some other objective. As you'll learn in the upcoming chapters, while creating a goal is an important first step, desire alone isn't going to bring results.

You need a strategy, a carefully laid plan, to bring about your desired outcome. Without a plan, you run the risk of letting things happen randomly, by chance or by accident. And if you just go along letting life happen at will, you never know how things will turn out. Maybe it will be just fine, and you'll be happy with any outcome—be it job, friends, your living arrangements and the like. But maybe it will not be to your liking, and you'll feel disappointed, short-changed—or worse. Probably you've heard any number of people say, "If only I had . . ." Don't let yourself get caught in the "shoulda, coulda, woulda" category.

Planning is the key to getting what you want. You "direct" the outcome of your life by the things you do—and don't do—each day. So have a plan. If you don't anticipate ahead of time what you are going to wear to school tomorrow, you might get up and find that a favorite item or outfit needs to be laundered and therefore you'll have to choose something else, something that is not "the look" for which you hoped. But if you plan, you can see if your clothes are clean and ready to wear. If you are taking a friend to a birthday dinner at his or her favorite restaurant, and you don't call ahead for reservations, you may get there and find that you cannot be seated (or arrive and find you've chosen the one day the restaurant is closed). Of course, by planning, you can avoid these things.

Create Your Map

A plan to achieve your goals serves as your map, showing you the exact route for getting to your destination—which is succeeding in accomplishing your goals. In the next chapter, you'll learn ten "rules" for creating goals, guidelines that will increase your chances of following through on achieving the things you'd like to accomplish. Then, you'll get a chance to formulate goals in nine specific categories—which is sure to help you feel like you're living life to its fullest! And, you'll learn how to create a plan of action to achieve each of those goals and see how doing so is a terrific way to manage your time.

And speaking of managing your time, how are you doing it? Do you feel you're meeting your schedule, or do you often feel behind or overwhelmed? Do you seem to never have enough time?

_____

_____

If not having enough time seems to be a problem for you, why do you think this is so? Do you think it's because you simply have too much to do, or is it because of the way you prioritize your activities?

_____

_____

Do you lose control over getting things done when they need to be accomplished? Or do you sometimes procrastinate, putting things off until the last minute, until you are faced with the mad rush to get things done?

_____

_____

If you constantly battle with knowing what needs to be done now as opposed to what can be done later, or even much later? You'll learn how to better manage your time in the upcoming chapters.

CHAPTER 10
Ten Important Rules for Designing Great Goals

This Year Things Are Going to Be (Really) Different!

This next year, I'm going to do things a lot differently than I did last year. I know I said this last year, but having really blown it, I am positively sure I'm changing my ways this next school year. And for good reason!

Last year as I was getting ready to go into ninth grade, I thought, Okay, this is my first year being in high school, and I want to get off to a good start. I'm going to be cool this year, and I'm going to accomplish some things. I want to make a lot of great friends and have everyone at school think of me as someone who's really got it together.

I'm going out for sports; I'm going to find a cool boyfriend; be elected as an officer of my class; and please my parents by getting good grades. I want to look and act cool. I especially want to grow my hair long, and I'm going to work out to my aerobics video every single day. I had some other goals, too. For example, I'd promised myself, no more swearing, and just to make sure I wouldn't, I decided I would stop hanging around with Randee Hogan. Not only does she cuss all the time, but she's a big gossip and I should know:

Last year I'd gotten in more than my share of sticky situations by getting caught up in the rumors she started—like the one about Sierra Gould making out with Tristin Tyler. You can't believe how much my reputation was tarnished because I hung around with her (and because everyone knew the rumor wasn't true). So I knew some changes were in order, and now that I'd become a ninth-grader, I decided that there would be no more spreading gossip and rumors for me, because I had decided that it was "out" with Randee, and "in" with Shandra Gregory and Wendy Tomposa, the best-liked and most-respected girls at school. To all these great intentions, I'd start doing something really cool with my soon-to-be-long, flowing hair—which is really saying something, since my hair is, as my best friend says, a "problem child with a mind of its own."

My ninth-grade year started, and before I knew it, it was over, and quite frankly, I didn't know whether to laugh or cry at how it turned out. First, I spent the whole year waiting for Nathan Baker to notice me, and what a waste of time that was! He didn't even notice that I was alive—although Lenny Stone did. He asked me out, but I said "no," which was a dumb decision because he's cool and one of the best-liked guys in the school. (I was just holding out for Nathan.) I wasted my entire year waiting for Nathan and only Nathan, who was dating Sara Goldman, a girl two years older than he. I was so sure that sooner or later, they'd break up—but they're still together.

On the matter of my grades . . . well, my parents were hardly deliriously happy with them—although I was happy just to pass: It seemed like there was one homework assignment on top of another, and I was always behind and turning assignments in late on a regular basis—which got me a lower grade every time, so I'm just glad I'm going into tenth grade!

As for my working out, well, I broke out the aerobics videotape all of three times the entire school year; I never did decide on a new hairstyle; and as for my friendships with Shandra and Wendy, well, they're still waiting to be developed. With my keeping tabs on Nathan and his girlfriend, and constantly checking around on the status of their relationship, I lost a lot of precious time. I guess you could say that was true for the time I spent with Randee, too.

I ended up hanging around with her for most of the year, so my goal of not hanging out with her and instead spending time with "nicer" friends bit the dust, as did most of all my other goals. At least I still managed to cut down on the swearing a little bit.

In my ninth-grade year, I didn't get all the things accomplished that I'd hoped. Now as I'm getting ready to go into the tenth grade, I'm not going to leave things to "hope." This year I'm going to write my goals down and put them where I can see them. After last year, when the time just got away from me, this year I plan to be very serious about making sure things hap- pen according to plan! —**Cammie Brinthall, 15**

"The Rules" for Designing Goals (You'll Commit To)

Do you, like Cammie, start out with great intentions, but then get sidetracked from accomplishing the things you want to get done? It can happen. But it's a lot less likely to happen if you have a plan for achieving the things you want to accomplish. With a plan, things aren't left to chance. If you know the direction in which you should head, you know where to focus your time and energy. Channeling your efforts in a specific direction can keep you on track to getting what you want, to bringing your intentions to fruition.

But although goals may start out as hopes, dreams, desires, intentions or ambitions, they are more than wishful thinking. Goals are concrete plans. Here are ten "rules" for creating goals, guidelines that will increase your chances of following through on achieving the things you'd like to accomplish. (In the coming chapters, you'll get a chance to learn more about each of these and create a plan of action that leads to your achieving your goals.)

1. **Put your goals in writing**. Writing out your goals helps you examine them and see what they really are. Doing this can help you commit to them. Once you've written out those things you'd like to "do, be, have and achieve," you have a "map" reminding you of where you wish to be—and when you wish to arrive there. Knowing when and where you want to be helps you develop a plan, so you know how best to spend your time and energy. This can help you stay on track toward accomplishing the things you want to achieve.

   A plan points you in the direction of what it is you should be doing each month, week and day to move closer to your goal. And best of all, with a written plan, you can readily see all you are doing. You can measure how far you've come, and when you are off course. Then you can get back to doing those things that move you in the direction of meeting your goals. Notice that Cammie, in the story at the beginning of this chapter, had many goals, but she never wrote them down. As you can see, the goals she professed became merely good intentions. If Cammie had written down her goals, her intentions would have been trans- formed into a plan of action, and as a result, she would have had a better chance at goal achievement.

2. **Be sure your goal is clear and specific**. Goals that are specific, as opposed to those that are ambiguous, are easier to tackle. State your goals clearly and be specific. For example, rather than saying, "I need to make some money," say, "I need to make at least sixty-five dollars each month between now and Christmas."

   If Cammie had selected one specific sport, rather than just saying, "I want to go out for sports," she would have had a better chance of knowing precisely when she needed to "sign up and show up" to begin achieving her goal. As it was, her goal was never clear: She didn't clarify what sport she wanted to go out for, and the result was that Cammie had no direction— no beginning and no end. She never did become part of any sports team during her ninth-grade year. If you don't decide a direction in which to go, it's unlikely you'll reach your desired destination—such as was true for Cammie in her ninth-grade school year.

3. "<u>Own</u>" <u>your goal(s)</u>. When you set a goal, ask, "Is this goal really important to me?" If you don't really "buy into" your goal—if you don't really want to accomplish it—it's unlikely that you will make the commitment to see it through. As an example, if your parents want you to be a good student, and if you view being a good student and getting good grades as something you do more for some- one else rather than for yourself (as was true for Cammie), then you may not be as serious in pursuing that goal. You have to say and believe, "Meeting this goal is important to ME." When you set a goal, own it. Write it in such a way that you believe both in the goal and in your desire to achieve it.

4. <u>Be sure your goal is realistic—and attainable</u>. There is a direct relationship between how much you believe your goal is one you can attain and your accomplishing it. For example, if you are taking a foreign-language class that requires you to memorize two hundred words for a final, and you intend to accomplish this the evening prior to the final—unless you're a real language genius, it could well be an impossible feat. But, if you break the list into a certain number of words per day per week and give yourself, say, one to two weeks to memorize them, it's more likely you'll achieve your goal.

5. <u>Break your goals down into manageable tasks</u>. Breaking a goal into manageable tasks, and listing the activities necessary to achieve each of them, can be very helpful in accomplishing the smaller activities that lead to your big- ger goal. (You'll learn more about this in the next chapter.) For example, getting into college may be one of your long- range goals, but no doubt, there are any number of things you'll need to do along the way—such as doing well in each of your classes; taking all the required entrance exams; sending for applications, filling them out and returning them; even doing things such as arranging for tuition, text- books, room and board, and so on.

6. <u>Decide on the timeline for your goals</u>. Do you have yearly, monthly, weekly and daily goals? Like Cammie, who set her goals at the beginning of the school year, you, too, may decide to frame your goals within a school year. Or you may decide to set your goals in accordance with a calendar year, such as January 1 to December 31. Many adults use the calendar year, while many students, like Cammie, use the school year as a timeline for goal achievement. You may even opt to go month-

to-month. Whatever you choose is up to you. What's important is that you give yourself a timeline to "house" your long-term and short-term goals. Thinking of your life in bigger chunks of time (such as a school term, as opposed to simply living day-to-day), will give you a better chance of meeting long-range goals.

Many goals (like doing well during the school year and planning for college) require a longer period to accomplish. This also gives you a bigger span of time to measure your progress. If you set your timeline of goals within a school term, do so knowing precisely what month, even what week, you have targeted for completing tasks, all the while keeping in mind that each of these activities need to be accomplished in order to meet your larger goals.

7. <u>Set deadlines for completing each of your goals</u>. Having a completion date helps you prioritize where and how you will allocate (spend) your time. In meeting a goal, if something doesn't have to be done this week or this month, you know you have time for other things. If you're nearing a deadline, you can push yourself just a little harder. Perhaps if Cammie had given herself a deadline to get each of her goals completed, she might have fared better. As an example, if she had decided on a "cut-off point" for when she would no longer wait around for Nathan Baker and his girlfriend to break up (so that he would be eligible), she might have decided to accept Lenny Stone's (or someone else's) invitation to go out. Cammie didn't meet her goal of "having a boyfriend" during her ninth-grade year, because she didn't set a deadline to give up on waiting for the breakup.

8. <u>Keep a copy of your goal plan in sight</u>. Keeping your goals where you can refer to them on a regular basis is a great way to stay focused on what's "most" important to you, even as you go about the whirlwind of your daily activities. Many teens tape their goals on their mirror or keep them inside their day planner. This would have helped Cammie stay focused, but with nothing written down, she wasn't able to remain focused on those things she had professed were so important to her at the beginning of her school year. Consequently, Cammie failed to meet almost all her goals.

9. <u>Review and revise your goals periodically</u>. Regardless of your timeline—be it calendar year, school term or monthly goals—

review your goals periodically. Sometimes you need to add to your goals; for example, if you decide not to go to college and instead to attend a ten-month training program, you'll need to revise your plans. Or, if one of your goals is to be on a sports team and you sprain a ligament, maybe you need to revise your goal—and maybe a new goal for getting physical therapy will need to be added. Reviewing your goals allows you to measure your progress with each of them. Cammie didn't do this, and as a result, she didn't stop the days from "slipping away from her." Perhaps if she had taken the time to review and revise her goals regularly, she would have realized that not only was time slipping away, but so were her ideals for becoming all that she had hoped to be and do during her ninth-grade year.

10. <u>After completing a goal, reward yourself.</u> You have set a goal and accomplished it. Good for you! Accomplishing a goal is a good feeling. Goal achievement is also good for your self-esteem. When you accomplish what you set out to achieve you see yourself as capable, and you believe in your ability to be goal-oriented. You see yourself as the "winner" you are! When you achieve a goal, celebrate! Reward yourself by doing something nice for yourself! Maybe it's more time with friends or tickets to a special concert. Rewarding yourself is about showing yourself appreciation for a "mission accomplished." If Cammie had rewarded herself after each triumph (she did meet with some success when she worked out a few times and cut down on swearing), perhaps she would have been more motivated to stay in tune with her professed goals.

YOUR TURN: WHAT'S YOUR READ ON "THE RULES"?

Answer each of the following questions:

Why do you think it's important to set goals that are important to you?

_____

_____

Has there ever been a time when it was important to achieve a goal, but it wasn't one you "owned"? Whose goal was it? Did you achieve the goal?

_____

_____

Name a time you set a goal and it wasn't realistic. What was the goal? In what way was it not realistic? How did things turn out—did you achieve it or not? What did you learn from that experience?

_____

_____

Do you already post your goals where you can see them? If so, have you ever had friends (or family members) make a comment about your goals? What comments did they make?

_____

_____

Would you be embarrassed to post your goals in plain view— say, on the refrigerator, or on the mirror of your room, or on the wall next to where you study and do your homework?

_____

_____

How do you stay organized? Do you have a calendar or a day planner? If so, how long have you used it to order and prioritize your monthly, weekly and daily goals/projects/activities? How has doing this made a difference in your life?

_____

_____

Do any of your friends keep a day planner or use any other way of organizing their time and activities (such as a calendar where they can write in activities to complete and dates when they are due)? Explain.

_____

_____

Do you get an allowance? If so, is it tied to specific goals, such as keeping up your share of home responsibilities? What other rewards, if any, do you receive for meeting specific goals? Do you find these rewards motivating?

_____

_____

What sort of reward system do you think would work best to motivate you in reaching your goals? What sorts of rewards could you give yourself to celebrate your achievements?

_____

_____

Do you keep a log of your goals from grade to grade or year to year? How can doing that give you a sense of achievement?

_____

_____

What Sort of "Road Map" Do You Use To Set Goals?

Wandering aimlessly through a new town wouldn't be the most effective way to find a specific restaurant, shopping center, sports arena or whatever you were hoping to locate. Probably you'd do better using a map, or directions you'd been given or some sort of guide in finding your way around. The same is true in meeting your goals. By using the goal-setting guidelines, you now have a reliable compass to guide you where you want to go.

It's time for you to do some "destination" planning for yourself. So where do you want to go? Do most of your goals center around just your friends? Or, are they mostly about doing well in school? Do you set goals only in times when things are getting stressful—such as when a big paper is soon due? What motivates you to set goals?

One of the most important reasons to set goals is to minimize stress, and still do all the things you want and more. Ideally, your goals should be comprehensive enough to complement all areas of your life, as this next chapter will cover.

CHAPTER 11
Nine Goals for a "Full-On" Life

What Goals Have You Set for Yourself?

What is a "full-on" life? Let's think about that. When someone asks you what your goals are, generally they ask you about something. For instance, someone might ask you, "What are your career plans?" or "Have you given any thought to where you'd like to live when you're out of school?" But most likely you don't just have one key goal. If someone were to ask you what your single most important goal in life is, you'd probably have a difficult time answering the question. Maybe you would say something such as, "I want to be healthy, happy and successful," but it's such a broad statement, it seems vague and unclear.

One goal doesn't cover all the things you want to "do, have and be" in your life. What's important is that you set goals in several areas so that you, too, can have as Alan says, a "full-on" life. After all, you have a social life, an academic life, a family life, a spiritual life, and you need time for recreation and to earn the money you need to cover those things that are your responsibility to pay for. And, of course, you'll want to explore what you'd like to do for a job or career of your choice—among other things.

Accordingly, your goals should reflect a spectrum of areas, for example, plans for:
- Having good times and great relationships with parents, friends, teachers and others
- Preparing for what you'd like to do for work or career once you're out of school
- Caring for your spiritual wellness
- Satisfying your curiosity for things you would like to know more about
- Having a job to pay for things and to save for college and a car
- Staying fit and healthy
- Having the time for hobbies
- Gaining or maintaining respect from others

IDENTIFYING GOALS IN THESE 9 VERY IMPORTANT AREAS

You can design goals to help assure that you have a "full-on" life. The following categories (and explanations to stimulate thinking) are useful in planning living a vibrant and balanced life. Use these nine categories to set goals that help you feel that your life is full, exciting, and that you are not missing out on all the ways that you can be using your time to fully explore your talents, hobbies and natural abilities, as well as your beliefs and quest for your meaning, purpose and achievement in life.

The nine categories are:

1. SPIRITUAL GROWTH: What are your goals for peace of mind, search for meaning and spiritual fulfillment?

2. PERSONAL RELATIONSHIPS: What are your goals for enhancing your relationships (with parents, friends, teachers, others)?

3. LEARNING AND EDUCATION: What would you like to know more about? What skills do you want to develop?

4. STATUS AND RESPECT: To which groups/organizations/ associations or affiliations do you want to belong? From whom do you want respect?

5. LEISURE TIME AND HOBBIES: What activities (hobbies, sports, travels) would you like to learn more about (or to do more of)?

6. FITNESS AND HEALTH WELL-BEING: What are your goals for your physical fitness and overall health?

7. FINANCIAL: What are your goals for having enough money to do the things you want to do?

8. JOB AND CAREER: What kind of job would you like? What are your goals for productive work and career success?

9. COMMUNITY SERVICE AND SERVING OTHERS: What are your plans to do "good works" within your neighborhood and community, and to help others?

Alan Navarro's Goals

We asked Alan Navarro to show us his plan for accomplishing all the things he'd like to do during his school year. Here's how Alan listed his goals in each of these categories.

1. SPIRITUAL GROWTH: Goals: I'd like to pray each day; trust God to guide me through my trials; and always thank God for all the things for which I am grateful.

2. PERSONAL RELATIONSHIPS: Goals: I'd like to stay in touch with my mother, calling her whenever I can and writing her letters every week; and, to make time for my friends and tell my teachers thank-you for helping me get a good education. I'd like to find my father and get him back in my life.

3. LEARNING AND EDUCATION: Goals: I'd like to stay on the honor roll.

4. STATUS AND RESPECT: Goals: I'd like to join the Association for Collectibles and Memorabilia—and have members think of me as someone "in the know" (which I'll do by writing a story for them about how I set up my creative Web site).

5. LEISURE TIME AND HOBBIES: Goals: I'd like to learn how to snowboard.

6. FITNESS AND HEALTH WELL-BEING: Goals: I'd like to keep up my jogging at least five miles three times a week.

7. FINANCIAL: Goals: I'd like to continue to put aside a minimum of $150 each month for college from my job at the sporting goods store; I want to send Mom $100 for her birthday in two months.

8. JOB AND CAREER: Goals: Someday I'd like to run my own Web-based sports memorabilia trading company, so I want to learn all I can about sports trading cards and memorabilia, and about how to own and run a Web-based sports memorabilia trading company.

9. COMMUNITY SERVICE AND SERVING OTHERS: Goals: Continue to get Mrs. Larsen's prescription from Save-on and deliver it to her at the first of the month. Check out becoming a "Big Brother."

Reading over Alan's overall goals, you can see how they make his school year look full and complete. That's one of the many benefits of creating a list of overall goals for a significant length of time, such as the school year: It gives you a design for having a life that is as full and rich as you want it to be.

YOUR TURN: Identify Your Goals

You will want to create goals for yourself in each of these nine categories and set a time frame for accomplishing them. We suggest you use the timeline of a school year.

As you do this exercise, you may be thinking about your goals overall, for example, in the job/career category. Maybe you already know what you'd like to do for work. If, like Alan, who said he wanted to own his own Web-based sports memorabilia company, you know your overall goal in that area, remind yourself that while you may already know the overall goal, here your intent is to identify your goal within the time frame of a school year. That way, it will be more likely that you will be able to list the activities necessary for you to do this coming year to meet or further your overall goal.

1. SPIRITUAL GROWTH: What are your goals for peace of mind, search for meaning and spiritual fulfillment?

   _____

   _____

2. PERSONAL RELATIONSHIPS: What are your goals for enhancing your relationships (with parents, friends, teachers, others)?

   _____

   _____

3. LEARNING AND EDUCATION: What would you like to know more about? What skills do you want to develop?

   _____

   _____

4. STATUS AND RESPECT: To which groups/organizations/ associations or affiliations do you want to belong? From whom do you want respect?

   _____

5. LEISURE TIME AND HOBBIES: What activities (hobbies, sports, travels) would you like to learn more about (or to do more of)?

    _____

    _____

6. FITNESS AND HEALTH WELL-BEING: What are your goals for your physical fitness and overall health?

    _____

    _____

7. FINANCIAL: What are your goals for having enough money to do the things you want to do?

    _____

    _____

8. JOB AND CAREER: What kind of job would you like? What are your goals for productive work and career success?

    _____

    _____

9. COMMUNITY SERVICE AND SERVING OTHERS: What are your plans to do "good works" within your neighborhood and community, and to help others?

    _____

    _____

Whether your goals are long-range or short-range, you'll be better able to achieve your goals if you break them down into manageable parts so that you can do the things necessary in order to get to the next step. For example, before Alan can start selling his sports memorabilia, he'll need to set up a website. The next chapters will explain how.

CHAPTER 12

Breaking Your Goals into a Manageable "To-Do" List

Some goals, such as to become a scientist or to have a wonderful family (or, as in a previous story, to become a substance abuse counselor), are big, bold and ambitious—or, as Jordanne said, "Eiffel Tower plans." Many times the accomplishment of goals, especially those that are broad and long-range, requires that you take lots of steps in between in order to move you toward your bigger goal. This is true for plans for the future, such as going to college—which means that you'll want to do things such as get good grades year by year in order to meet your overall goal of getting accepted into a college of your choice.

Goals are easier attained when they're broken down into manageable tasks.

It helps if you prioritize your larger overall goals into monthly activities and then into weekly and daily to-do's.

Listing what needs to be done and when it needs to be completed will help you get things done without feeling overwhelmed—which may mean you will then abandon your goal.

But it is important to write things down, to make a list of activities, your to-do's that need to be done and when you want those accomplished. If you can see "at a glance" what needs to be done and in a certain frame so you can focus on that and not worry about the rest. Prioritizing your activities helps you stay organized and in charge of your time.

List the goals you'd like to accomplish in the span of your school year. Then, break those into monthly goals.

Set goals in each of the nine categories. In the beginning, if this seems a little overwhelming, you can begin with two or three areas. Then, when you can see how easy this method of breaking your goals into manageable parts is, you can add on until you have developed goals in all nine categories. Whether you set one goal or many, think about what must be done this month, then break your goals into the activities you want to accomplish for each month.

The next thing is to break your monthly goals into weekly to-do's.

Breaking Your Monthly Goals into Weekly "To-Do's"

You're more likely to accomplish your goal if you make a list of what needs to be done for the month at hand, and then create activities into what needs to be done on a weekly basis.

We asked Tyanna to share with us her goals for the month. She listed one month's activities as:

- Help 3 friends have a B-day party for Sienna
- Complete the big history project
- Make at least $75
- Go to Valentine's Day dance (with Kevin!)
- Go to church 4 times
- Keep all my grades up.

Now, Tyanna will need to break these goals into weekly activities. We asked her to share one week of her monthly goals.

Goals for Week #1
1. Call the four families I baby-sit for, and let them know I'm available and "looking for work"
2. Call Grams and ask her for money for my B-day instead of some other gift
3. Talk to Brittany and Kendahl about having a B-day party for Sienna
4. Make invitations to Sienna's B-day party
5. Get to school early on Thurs: Kevin has band practice—hang out with Brit near band room
6. Need to start my big paper! Check out library reference books for history project
7. Go to church Thurs. eve service with Kendahl
8. Ask Brit if she'll hand off my letter to Kevin asking if he's going to ask me to the Valentine's Day school dance

Making—and accomplishing—a weekly to-do list can help you stay on track toward meeting your goals. As you check off those things you've accomplished, and check to see what's coming up, you can see how you're spending your time in a balanced, worthwhile way.

A sense of accomplishment is always a good feeling, and one that contributes to your feeling positive about yourself—in other words, you gain a reputation with yourself as a doer, an achiever and someone who is taking charge of his or her life. The result adds to a healthy self-esteem.

The next step: breaking your weekly tasks into daily to-do's.

CREATING YOUR DAILY TO-DO LISTS

My Snake Is Missing: Have You Seen It?

A couple of weeks ago, my family and I were staying at a cabin in the mountains. One day I saw a sleek and beautiful four-foot gopher snake. The snake noticed me and rather than hurrying away edged a little closer, like it was curious about me. I stood there talking to it and sure enough, the snake did want to make my acquaintance! Being rather friendly, it slithered my way, close enough for the two of us to get a good look at each other. I leaned down, picked it up, and within moments the gorgeous creature wrapped her pretty self around my arm. I swear that snake purred while it enjoyed the warmth of my skin. I told her I'd sure like to take her home with me, and I thought she smiled at me—like she was pleading with me to let her live in an aquarium in my house. "Done deal!" I assured her. "You are now my pet."

Of course, I asked Dad if I could take it home first. He said, "As long as you are a responsible pet owner." I swore I would be. But heck, I wanted that snake and would promise anything to have her. Are you with me on this?

I put my new pet in a paper sack with vent-holes so she'd have air, placed her in the trunk for her ride to her new home, and off we went. Well, having been a pet owner for all of two hours, how was I to remember there was a snake in our trunk? Our family reached home, and everyone was unpacking the car. I opened the trunk and started taking out things, when suddenly two red reptilian eyes lurched at me. The next thing I heard was the thud of my back hitting the pavement, and I lay gasping for air. I mean, I've never been so scared in all my life. Scrambling to my feet I yelled, "I'll unpack the trunk!" I quickly got everything out, looking for the snake as I did. It was nowhere to be found. So, thinking it needed a little time to calm down—like I did—I closed the trunk and went to the fridge to get something to eat and have time to regroup from my panic attack. About twenty minutes later I returned to search for my new pet.

I looked and looked, but simply couldn't find that reptile. I decided it needed more time to come out of its hiding place. Several hours later when everyone was unpacked and our family was buzzing with the normal activities of home, Dad asked, "How's that snake adjusting, Son? Did you get her all set up in the aquarium?"

"Well, Dad," I told him (I mean, he was coming down the hall to my room, and I'd neither set up the aquarium nor located my snake, so it wasn't like I didn't have to level with him about my snake being missing), "just one small problem. She's still sleeping in the car, so I didn't want to disturb her."

"She's where?" he yelled. "Let's get that &?!#% snake out of my car, NOW!"

"Sure thing, Dad!" I said, following my dad who was nearly on a run to the garage. We couldn't find the snake. We even took out the mat, the spare tire and all the tire tools. So then, thinking the snake had found a hole and crawled into the back seat of the car, we searched the back seat, too. We looked everywhere including under the seats, and then in and around the front seats. That snake wasn't in any of these places. "I'll get a flashlight," my dad barked and strode into the house to get one. The next sounds I heard was my sister screaming and my dad consoling my mother. "No, the snake can't be on the loose in the house, it's still somewhere in the car—or the garage." My dad returned with the flashlight and searched the entire car again. And then, stretched out across the entire front seat, he searched under the dashboard— where he discovered the snake, coiled around all those cute colored wires, and in none-too-good of a snake-mood either. The minute the beam from Dad's flashlight hit that snake's eyes, it HISSSSSED loud enough, it seemed, for the neighbors to hear. Frightened out of his wits, my dad let out a blood-curdling yell and rolled out of the car so fast you wouldn't believe it.

"He's on the wires," my dad said and then barked, "Get that #@!?# snake out of my car!" Guess he wasn't wild about a snake being within millimeters of his femoral artery. Believing the snake was just minutes away from my putting her in the aquarium, my dad left the scene. But here's the thing: While my dad and I were having our panic attack, the snake had slithered off to a new hiding place. I searched every inch of the car and the garage, but the snake had vanished into thin air. Luckily, and surprisingly, no one in my family asked me about the snake that night. What a relief that was! Maybe it was because on my way to my room that evening, I announced, "Good night, everybody! I've got a huge test tomorrow and need to hit the books!" Having said that, I closed the door to my room and didn't come out again.

I did my homework and went to bed, but I didn't get much sleep that night. I kept thinking about the moment when the light hit that snake's eyes, and they lit up as it hissed. It was such a "dangerous" sound. So around midnight, I got up to search for the snake, but once again, no luck. I went back to bed, deciding that I'd get up early the next day to check for the snake—but it never happened. Still tired, I got up later than I'd planned and, running late, I barely got myself together for school, let alone to have time to go search for the snake. When my mom called, "I'm leaving! Anyone not in the car in the next two minutes doesn't get a ride to school," I grabbed my books and headed for the car—praying that the snake was still in there, but that no one would sit on it or discover it in any way.

I'd promised myself that the moment school let out, I'd head straight for home and search for the snake in the garage. But my friends all suggested we go get smoothies at our favorite place at a nearby mall, so I totally forgot about my plans to find the snake. Next, we played some pool, one thing led to another and by the time I got home, I'd completely forgotten until I saw everyone in my family. They looked so "comfy" and content that I didn't have the heart to let them know the snake was still on the loose. I just let it go for the night, once again promising myself that I'd find that snake first thing the next morning—or after school, one of the two. But on Tuesday I woke up late and had to dash off, and after school I had football practice. Then my friend Kevin asked me to go help him download some tunes. By the time I got home, my parents were camped out in the living room watching television, and my sister was in the kitchen trying to make cupcakes for a classmate's birthday party at school the next day. It really wasn't possible to go rummaging through the car without letting on that it was because I hadn't yet found the snake.

On Wednesday I went to watch Lexi Johnson try out for a part in a play. She asked me to be there and, well, I've been crazy about Lexi all year and once she asked me to be there, nothing else entered my mind—including the missing reptile. By Thursday, I wasn't even thinking "snake," I mean, it's not like she'd become a member of the family or anything. Nor had I grown attached to her: I hadn't seen her for days! One thing having led to another, Saturday arrived before I remembered: The snake was still on the loose—either in some remote location in the family car or slithering around in the garage, or maybe it had escaped the garage and had crawled back to the mountain by now. Maybe it had even starved to death!

My pet snake has been missing for six days, and I didn't have the nerve to tell anyone in the house. I mean, if my mother knew, she'd put the house up for sale! That is, if she managed to live through the horror of it. And I don't even want to consider the consequences from my dad: the car, the free gas, all the privileges I've earned to spend time with my friends on weekends—all would be taken away for who knows how long. As for my sister, she would faint dead away—along with her little friends (who I swear live at our house more than their own). So, I can't let on that the snake is missing, though it can't be much longer until Dad comes into my room to look at the snake.

I don't have to worry about my sister or my mom. Both are terrified of snakes and have no desire to pay a visit to my room—where it isn't, at least not yet. But I'm so afraid that one of them is going to find that snake while in the garage (because that's where I assume it's hiding out). I must find the snake before the snake finds someone else, and one of my family members dies of a heart attack when they're greeted by a surprise run-in with the snake. And I really don't want the poor thing to die from not having had a meal in over a week (though maybe it's been eating mice, who knows?).

The bottom line is that finding that snake is something I absolutely must do! I just keep forgetting, or something else comes up that seems more urgent (at least at the time). I've seen notes my mom leaves to herself around the house, lists of reminders: "Pick up dry cleaning . . . Call dentist to schedule kids' checkups . . . Buy trash bags . . . PTA meeting at 6:00 . . ." While I always jot down my goals for the week, with all the trouble I seem to be having with getting around to my snake-hunt, I wonder if I need a daily reminder, something that says, "Urgent: Find snake TODAY!" —**Colin Sinclair, 18**

The Daily To-Do List

Does it sound to you as if it's a wise decision for Colin to make a to-do list with "find my snake—today!" at the very top of it? We think so, and we're hoping he did find the snake before his family did—or before it died from starvation!

How about you? Do you start your week promising yourself you're going to get so much accomplished but then, well, life happens (as Colin found out) and before you know it, the week is over, and you didn't accomplish all you'd hoped? It can happen. Does it happen to you?

Do you find that you start the week with great intentions, but then get sidetracked with a million-and-one things to do? That's the importance of a daily to-do list. It gives you the list of things you must get done today right there in black and white—bar none. While you may put the usual things on your list, such as classes or regularly scheduled sports practice or any extra-curricular activities you attend, your daily to-do list should also include those things to get done from the goals you created within nine key categories.

To create your daily to-do list, begin by reviewing your goals for the week at hand. Then at the start of each day, or the prior evening, review your goals for the upcoming day so you are prepared for what greets you. This way, you know what you need to do to stay on course for the day. This is helpful because it allows you to gather up the necessary books or get permission slips signed by your parents and so on, so you can be as "on top of things" as possible. With your sights clearly set, you can then create a daily to-do list accordingly.

Colin has a busy schedule that includes doing well in his classes, working at his part-time job, and spending time with his family and friends as well as with his girlfriend. He's also on the football team, which meets for regular practices.

All those things should be reflected on his daily to-do list. But as you know from reading his story, Colin's weekly goals also need to reflect the "emergency" he's having—locating the snake he brought from the mountains hoping to house in an aquarium in his room.

Colin's WeeklyGoals

We asked Colin to share his goals for the upcoming week with us. Here's his week's agenda:

Goals for This Week
- Find snake !!!!!!!!!!!!!!!!!!!!!!!!!!!!!!!!!!!!!!!
- Ask Lexi to the school dance
- Pass algebra test
- Make $$$$ (for Friday dance and to buy mice for my snake)
- Mail recommendations for football scholarship: University of Nebraska and University of Iowa

Colin's Goals for Monday

Next, we asked Colin to break those weekly goals into daily to-do's. Here's his agenda for Monday:

Monday To-Do's
- FIND MY FRIGIN SNAKE!!!!!!!!!!!!!!!!!!!!!!!!!!!!!!!!!!
- Set alarm clock to get up early and go search tool cabinets in garage for snake
- Turn in my late algebra assignment
- Sit with Lexi at lunch
- Come straight home from school and search laundry area for snake
- Investigate "snake traps" (call pet store for safe ideas)
- Text Kenny and ask him to come over and help me look for my snake
- Start studying for Wednesday's test

Glancing at your daily to-do's at the beginning of the week can help remind you of the "easy" days, and those challenging days when need to be super prepared. And here's a suggestion: Don't toss these out. Keep them in a folder and refer to them when needed. They'll make for a great log of your activities. Try it; you'll see!

Goals don't mean you're "burdened" with things to do, as much as knowing what you need to do in a given time so that you master your bigger goals. And, be sure to put all the fun stuff on your list—plans for social time with friends, and time for keeping yourself healthy and fit and happy!

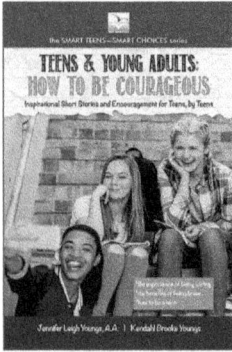

How to Be Courageous
Encouragment and Inspirational Short Stories by Teens and Young Adults
Jennifer Leigh Youngs, A.A. | Bettie B. Youngs, Ph.D., Ed.D.

- *the importance of being courageous*
- *the benefits of being brave*
- *how to be a hero*

Book: 978-1-940784-93-9
e-book: 978-1-940784-92-2

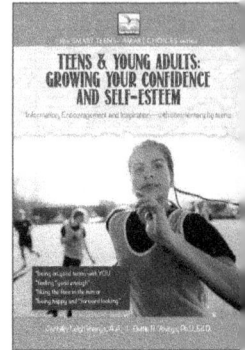

Growing Your Confidence and Self-Esteem
Information, Encouragement and Inspirational Short Stories by Teens and Young Adults
Jennifer Leigh Youngs, A.A. | Bettie B. Youngs, Ph.D., Ed.D.

- *being on good terms with YOU*
- *feeling "good enough"*
- *the power of confience*
- *liking the face in the mirror*
- *being happy and "forward looking"*

Book: 978-1-940784-86-1
e-book: 978-1-940784-87-8

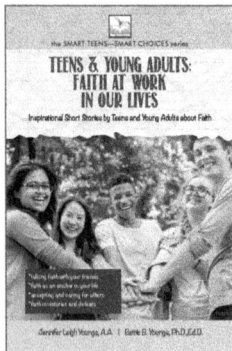

Faith at Work in Our Lives
Information, Encouragement and Inspirational Short Stories by Teens and Young Adults
Jennifer Leigh Youngs, A.A. | Bettie B. Youngs, Ph.D., Ed.D.

- *talking faith with your friends*
- *faith as an anchor in your life*
- *accepting and caring for others*
- *faith in victories and defeats*

Book: 978-1-940784-78-6
e-book: 978-1-940784-79-3

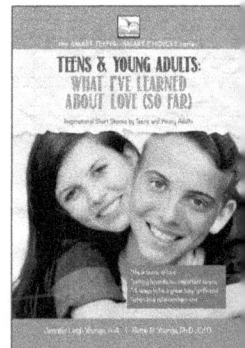

What I've Learned About Love (So Far)
Inspirational Short Stories by Teens and Young Adults
Jennifer Leigh Youngs, A.A. | Bettie B. Youngs, Ph.D., Ed.D.

- *the lessons of love*
- *setting boundaries important to you*
- *4 ways to be a great boy/girlfriend*
- *when love relationships end*

Book: 976-1-940784-75-5
e-book: 976-1-940784-74-8

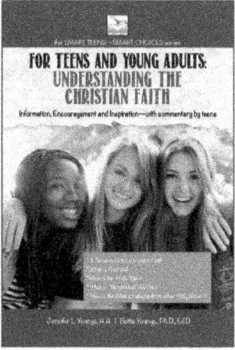

Understanding the Christian Faith

Information, Encouragement and Inspirational Short Stories by Teens and Young Adults
Jennifer Leigh Youngs, A.A. | Bettie B. Youngs, Ph.D., Ed.D.

- *9 Tenants of the Christian Faith*
- *What is Free Will*
- *What is the Holly Spirit*
- *What is "Reap What You Sow"*
- *How is the Bible as unique from other Holy Books?*

Book: 978-1-940784-76-2
e-book: 978-1-940784-77-9

Friends

Information, Encouragement and Inspirational Short Stories by Teens and Young Adults
Jennifer Leigh Youngs, A.A. | Bettie B. Youngs, Ph.D., Ed.D.

- *friends: pizza for life!*
- *how to be a good friend*
- *making and keeping friends*
- *when friendships end*

Book:976-1-940784-73-1
e-book: 976-1-940784-72-4

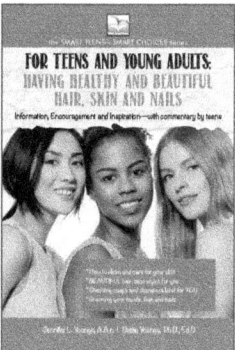

Having Healthy and Beautiful Hair, Skin and Nails

Information, Encouragement and Inspiration—with commentary by teens
Jennifer Leigh Youngs, A.A. | Bettie B. Youngs, Ph.D., Ed.D.

- *how to clean and care for your skin*
- *BEAUTIFUL hair; best styles for you*
- *choosing soaps and shampoos best for YOU*
- *grooming your hands, feet, and nails*

Book: 978-1-940784-84-7
e-book: 978-1-940784-85-4

The Power of Being Kind, Courteous and Thoughtful

Information, Encouragement and Inspirational Short Stories by Teens and Young Adults
Jennifer Leigh Youngs, A.A. | Kendahl Brooke Youngs

- *the power of being KIND*
- *the importance of being COURTEOUS*
- *how to be "THOUGHTFUL"*

Book: 978-1-940784-82-3
e-book: 978-1-940784-83-0

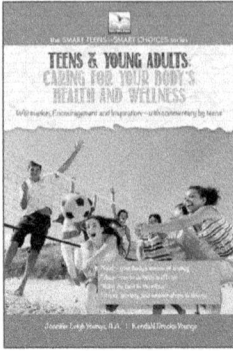

Caring for Your Body's Health and Wellness

Information, Encouragement and Inspirational Short Stories by Teens and Young Adults
Jennifer Leigh Youngs, A.A. | Bettie B. Youngs, Ph.D., Ed.D.

- *food—your body's source of energy*
- *sleep—restores body and brain*
- *liking the face in the mirror*
- *stress, anxiety, and emotional ups and downs*

Book: 978-1-940784-88-5
e-book: 978-1-940784-89-2

How to Have a Great Attitude

Information, Encouragement and Inspirational Short Stories by Teens and Young Adults
Jennifer Leigh Youngs, A.A. | Bettie B. Youngs, Ph.D., Ed.D.

- *food—your body's source of energy*
- *sleep—restores body and brain*
- *liking the face in the mirror*
- *stress, anxiety, and emotional ups and downs*

Book: 978-1-940784-90-8
e-book: 978-1-940784-91-5

TEEN TOWN PRESS
www.TeenTownPress.com

Teen Town Press

www.BettieYoungsBooks.com
info@BettieYoungsBooks.com

BYB
BETTIE YOUNGS BOOKS

AVAILABLE ON-LINE · *INGRAM BOOK GROUP* · THE PUBLISHER

Bettie Youngs Publishing Co., Inc.
www.BettieYoungsBooks.com
info@BettieYoungs.com

Foreign Rights:
Sylvia Hayse Literary Agency, LLC
hayses@caat.com

www.ingramcontent.com/pod-product-compliance
Lightning Source LLC
Chambersburg PA
CBHW032106080426
42733CB00006B/446